Ten Days that Changed the Nation

Also by Stephen Pollard

DAVID BLUNKETT

A CLASS ACT: THE MYTH OF BRITAIN'S
CLASSLESS SOCIETY
(with Andrew Adonis)

TEN DAYS
THAT CHANGED
THE NATION

The Making of Modern Britain

STEPHEN POLLARD

SIMON &
SCHUSTER

London · New York · Sydney · Toronto

A CBS COMPANY

First published in Great Britain by Simon & Schuster UK Ltd, 2009
A CBS COMPANY

1 3 5 7 9 10 8 6 4 2

Simon & Schuster UK Ltd
1st Floor
222 Gray's Inn Road
London WC1X 8HB

www.simonandschuster.co.uk

Simon & Schuster Australia
Sydney

A CIP catalogue record for this book is available
from the British Library.

ISBN: 978-1-84737-109-6

Typeset by M Rules
Printed in the UK by CPI Mackays, Chatham ME5 8TD

To Sam

CONTENTS

ACKNOWLEDGEMENTS

I would like to thank my agent, Jonny Pegg, for guiding me through the metamorphosis from my original idea to this finished product, and my editor, Katherine Stanton, not just for offering only constructive criticism but for doing so when she disagreed with much of what I wrote. But most of all I would like to thank my wife, Sam, without whom this book could not have been written.

INTRODUCTION

There are all sorts of theories of history. Some historians look for a sweeping narrative. Some stress the impact of individual men and women. Some look at social trends. Some look only at economics. All are, in their way, valid approaches.

But the events of just one day can also be critical. They can be both symbolic of a wider trend and powerful enough on their own to change the course of history. When, for instance, Neville Chamberlain resigned as Prime Minister in 1940, Lord Halifax rather than Winston Churchill was his preferred replacement. But on the key afternoon when the decision was taken, Halifax chose to go to the dentist. As one of the characters in Alan Bennett's play *The History Boys* puts it: 'If Halifax had had better teeth, we might have lost the war.'

Although Halifax's dental work falls outside my scope, I have approached the post-war history of Britain in much the same vein, analysing the impact of one key event across ten areas of national life. On the days I describe, something changed – something which, at the time, might have seemed insignificant but which, with hindsight, was of fundamental importance to our nation's development.

I have avoided the more obviously pivotal days – joining the then Common Market, Margaret Thatcher's election victory, or the day the contraceptive pill first went on sale, for example. Instead, I have tried to show how seemingly intractable problems or areas of national triumph have hinged not on great forces of history but on one, often apparently small, decision or event.

Not everyone will agree with my choice of areas to examine – immigration, the arts, education, food, politics, the monarchy, crime, football, radical Islam and the family – let alone the days I argue changed everything, but that is half the point. If you think I am wrong, for instance, to argue that the fatwa decreed against Sir Salman Rushdie for writing *The Satanic Verses* was a pivotal moment in history, then why do you think not? Was something else more important in the battle to preserve Western values? Or are they not threatened at all? Hopefully, at the very least, my choices will make you think about what has mattered in the decades since VE Day, even if they enrage – or amuse – you at the same time.

1

IMMIGRATION

22 June 1948

It is something of an irony that the ship which changed the face of Britain was a Nazi troop carrier.

On 22 June 1948, the SS *Empire Windrush* docked at Tilbury in Essex with 492 West Indians on board. Its arrival was a seminal moment in the history of modern Britain, marking the point at which we turned from being a mono-cultural, almost wholly white-skinned nation with a smattering of immigrants to one which was cosmopolitan, multi-ethnic and the home of mass immigration. The '*Windrush* generation' who travelled over in 1948 changed the very nature of British society. Throughout the 1950s they were followed by large-scale immigration – often ignored in the immigration debates which began in the 1960s – from Europe. These new workers came from Central and Eastern Europe, mainly Germany, Italy, Poland, Austria and Ukraine.

The *Monte Rosa* – the ship later renamed the *Empire Windrush* – was launched on 4 December 1930 in Hamburg by its builders, Blohm & Voss, as a diesel-powered cruise ship. With the rise to power of the Nazis, she became the favoured ship of high-ranking party officials and those they considered worthy of reward for services to the Third Reich. At the start of the Second World War, she was transferred to use as a barracks ship, first at the Polish port of Stettin and then as a troop carrier for Operation Weserübung, the German invasion of Norway in April 1940. Stationed in the north of Norway, she became an accommodation ship attached to the *Tirpitz*, the *Bismarck*'s sister ship. At the end of the war, as Germans started fleeing the Red Army in East Prussia and Danzig, she was used as an evacuation ship.

Back in German waters at Kiel, in May 1945 the *Monte Rosa* was seized by the Allies and then handed over to the British Ministry of Transport. On 21 January 1947 she was renamed HMT *Empire Windrush* and, run by the New Zealand Shipping Company on behalf of the British government, was put to service carrying troops between Southampton, Gibraltar, Suez, Aden, Colombo, Singapore and Hong Kong. Over the years in which she ran this route – extended after the start of the Korean War to Kure in Japan – she made one other journey, in 1948: from Australia to the UK, via Kingston, Jamaica. It was this one extra journey which was to have such a transformative impact on British society.

Even before the arrival of the *Empire Windrush* there had been a long history of emigration from the Caribbean. In the first half of the twentieth century, 150,000 Jamaicans left for the USA (mainly to nearby Florida) and Central America (to Panama to help build the Canal). The Second World War stepped up the level of emigration, although not to the USA where new laws banned seasonal workers. Previously, emigration had been dependent on above-average skills or energy and a capital investment to make departure and settling in elsewhere possible. The massive manpower requirements of the armed forces, however, ended such restraints. The Caribbean offered little in the way of prospects; joining up meant that a new world of opportunity could open elsewhere. Worse still, in August 1944 a hurricane had wreaked havoc on the already poor Jamaican infrastructure. Thousands of people were made homeless, the banana, coconut and coffee crops were destroyed and the economy was devastated, with unemployment running at over 25 per cent.

Although Britain was thought of as the 'Mother Country' and still ruled directly over the islands, travel between the Caribbean and Britain was difficult. There were no regular ships and those routes that were available were expensive, usually necessitating a trip to New York and thence to Britain. After the war ended, however, this changed. Former troop ships started collecting and depositing ex-servicemen – and some civilians – across the Empire. The first of these to visit the Caribbean was the *Empire Windrush* in 1948.

Servicemen from the Caribbean often took their leave back home. With the travel difficulties between the West Indies and Great Britain, it was decided to divert a ship to Jamaica to make a collection of 60 West Indian Royal Air Force servicemen. The ship's capacity was around 600. But there were less than 300 servicemen altogether to pick up. And so the ship's owners were given permission by the Ministry of Transport to offer the extra berths commercially. Three weeks before the *Empire Windrush* was due to dock in Jamaica on 24 May 1948, an advert appeared in the *Gleaner*, the main Jamaican newspaper. Three hundred one-way berths to Britain were advertised as available for £28 10s each. The response was almost instantaneous. Queues formed outside the booking agency and every place was sold.

One man's account is typical of the motivation for the passengers: 'When I went back to Jamaica [after being demobbed] it was shocking. Men who had been Home Guards, men who were working in the American factories and farms, men who were on the Panama Canal, and all of us, I would say 30,000 men, were thrown back without any planning. It was bad, and having examined the situation . . . I decided that my children would not grow up in a colony, so I came back [to Britain] on the SS *Empire Windrush* on 22 June 1948.'[1] That man was Sam King, a former pilot, who later became Mayor of Southwark in London. Speaking after his retirement as a councillor, he left no doubt about the effect of the *Empire Windrush*'s journey on his life: 'If I hadn't left I'd be a peasant farmer today . . . [M]y family had to sell three cows to raise the money [for me to leave]. To get papers to leave, a Justice of the Peace had to sign to say you were a responsible citizen and the police had to sign to say you were not a trouble maker.'[2]

In the years since the arrival of the *Empire Windrush*, during which time immigration has become more controversial, a myth has taken hold that the British government was responsible for bringing the passengers over as part of a concerted plan to help overcome a labour shortage: to do, as it is often put, 'the shit jobs'. But this is wrong. It is clear from the reaction of ministers that they were as surprised as the public when they first learned, via a telegram from the Acting Governor of Jamaica on 11 May, what was about to happen: 'I regret to inform you that more than 350 troop-deck passages by *Empire Windrush* . . . have been booked by men who hope to find employment in the United Kingdom, and that it is likely that this number will be increased by another 100 before the vessel leaves. Most of them have no particular skill and few will have more than a few pounds on their arrival.'[3] Reports of this passenger list soon started to filter through into the British press. The *Daily Express* reported on 8 June the reaction of George Isaacs, Minister of Labour: 'A shipload of worry for Mr George Isaacs, Minister of Labour, will arrive at Tilbury on Saturday week – 500 West Indians, all seeking jobs in Britain. Mr Isaacs confessed his worry to MPs yesterday. He said he does not know who sent the men. "All I know," he added, "is that they are in a ship and they are coming here. They are British citizens and we shall do our best for them when they arrive."'

But MPs did not allow the mystery of 500 British citizens to rest there. Hansard reports the questioning of George Isaacs:

> *Mr Stanley* (Tory: Bristol, W.) asked: Will you find out who is responsible for this extraordinary action?
>
> *Mr Isaacs*: That is already being done. I wish I knew, but I do not. Those who organised the movement of these

people to Britain did them a disservice in not contacting the Labour Ministry and giving it a chance to take care of them.

Mr Hughes (Socialist: Ayrshire, S.): Will you let them see the housing conditions in Scotland? Then they will want to go back to the West Indies.

Mr Driberg (Socialist: Maldon, Essex): Will you instruct your officials to meet the ship and help them find work in undermanned industries in the interests of production and welfare?

Mr Isaacs: They will be met at the ship and told how to register for employment. The arrival of these substantial numbers of men under no organised arrangements is bound to result in difficulty and disappointment. I have no knowledge of their qualifications or capacity and can give no assurance that they can be found suitable work. I hope no encouragement will be given to others to follow them.

In later years, the government did indeed set out on active recruitment campaigns. But these were precisely targeted with specific jobs in mind, rather than the general, unplanned, unexpected free-for-all of the *Empire Windrush's* passenger load. In April 1956, for instance, London Transport started a recruitment drive in Barbados. By 1968 it had taken on 3787 Barbadians,[4] lending them their fares to London. The NHS and British Rail had similar schemes. (Ironically, it was under Enoch Powell as Health Minister that the NHS launched one of its largest recruitment drives. Mr Powell then went on to spend the rest of his life bewailing immigration into the UK.)

The idea that the government was behind the arrival of the men on board the *Empire Windrush* is as mistaken as the opposing myth which is sometimes peddled: that the government, driven by racism, did everything in its power to stop the ship's arrival and then to make life so intolerable for the passengers that they would decide to go home. One report at the time had it that HMS *Sheffield*, a pocket battleship, was being sent on to the *Empire Windrush*'s path to frighten the captain away from docking. The rumour on board the *Empire Windrush* was that, as one passenger put it: 'If there was any disturbance on the immigrant ship, HMS *Sheffield* would be sent out to turn us back. I saw a man crying over the side because he thought we would be turned around.'[5] True, the *Sheffield* was in the vicinity of the *Empire Windrush* for a time, but that was mere coincidence. There were not just civilians on board, after all: there were also servicemen. The Colonial Secretary, Creech Jones, made it clear that: 'These people have British passports and they must be allowed to land.' Although he did then add, 'There's nothing to worry about because they won't last one winter in England.'[6]

The truth is that the government, caught by surprise, tried its best to smooth the arrival of the men on board but that the civil service seemed crippled by anxiety. Far from being racist, civil servants were clear that the men were British citizens and should be treated as such. In an internal Ministry of Labour memo dated 19 June 1948, it was made clear that:

There is no logical ground for treating a British subject who comes of his own accord from Jamaica to Great

Britain differently from another who comes to London on his own account from Scotland. Nevertheless public attention has been focused on the 400 or so men who are coming from Jamaica and who will arrive in London on Tuesday. A political problem has been created, to the embarrassment of the government and of our Minister in particular. In these circumstances it is necessary to see whether any extraordinary measures can be taken that would help solve the problem. If only they could be dispersed in small parties, then even though they did not get immediate employment, they would cease to be recognizable as a problem.[7]

Political problem they may have been but the Prime Minister, Attlee, was in no doubt about how to react. Responding to a round-robin letter sent to him by Labour MPs expressing their grave concern at the ship's arrival and floating the idea of repatriation – a note which can legitimately be said to be motivated in part by racism – Attlee wrote:

I note what you say, but I think it would be a great mistake to take the emigration of this Jamaican party to the United Kingdom too seriously. It is traditional that British subjects, whether of Dominion or Colonial origin (and of whatever race or colour), should be freely admissible to the United Kingdom. That tradition is not, in my view, to be lightly discarded, particularly at a time when we are importing foreign labour in large numbers . . . If our policy were to result in a great influx of undesirables, we might, however unwillingly, have to consider modifying it. But I would not be willing to consider that except on really compelling evidence, which I do not think exists at the present time.[8]

The Ministry of Labour, the Colonial Office and the local authorities may not have had long to put together a support mechanism for the arrivals but they did their best. The problems that greeted the passengers were ones of accident, not design. The civil service was simply thrown into apprehension and unease at such a departure from normality. As Mike and Trevor Phillips put it in their account of the *Windrush*'s impact:

> It was, after all, a service which, for the last decade, had run a tightly controlled, amazingly disciplined bureaucracy. Every aspect of life was subject to some form of control. Every last ounce of food was allocated and monitored. Every resource analysed and weighed. This was the real problem. The issue of race might have reinforced the civil servants' agitation, but their primary motivation was distress at the advent of a group of workers about whom they knew no details, whose movements were completely unregulated and who couldn't be controlled by official sanctions.[9]

That said, all the immigrants were briefed on arrival at Tilbury and each was given official documentation and classification – essential in post-war Britain. The *Daily Express* reported their arrival thus: 'Four hundred and fifty Jamaicans crowded the rails of the *Empire Windrush* as she anchored in the Thames last night. They sailed as refugees from their island's unemployment problem, and have provided a new problem to the Colonial Office and Ministry of Labour.' Loudspeakers called the 450 work-seekers to a pep talk by Mr Ivor Cummings, a principal officer of the Colonial Office, who welcomed them by telling them that things would not be easy.

Some of the men were resentful. But most appreciated the assistance they were given. As Sam King put it: 'We knew we were not wanted but, being British, once we arrived at Tilbury everything humanly possible was done to help us.'[10] Indeed, when they learned that the Colonial Office had only heard of their impending arrival twelve days earlier, most switched the blame to the Jamaican government.

After registering, they were taken to pre-arranged accommodation. Eighty-two of the men, who were joining the armed forces, were sent to a Wimpole Street hostel (costing them £1 1s a week); 104, who had friends or relatives in the UK – there was already a network of demobbed soldiers and airmen – were sent off to their contacts; and the rest were taken by coach to air-raid shelters on Clapham Common. The men housed in Clapham were given an official welcome at the Brixton Astoria by the local Mayor and three MPs. 'We want you to regard this country as your second home. I hope it will not be very long before each of you is provided for in a dignified fashion,' said Lt. Col. Lipton, the local MP, repeating a wish he had expressed earlier that day in the House of Commons. But, they were told by Tom Driberg, Britain was 'not a paradise. You have been warned that there may be difficulties caused through ignorance and prejudice, but don't let it get you down. Try and stand on your own feet as soon as you can.'[11]

The shelters were not too bad. There was a large welfare effort, both official and unofficial. The Women's Voluntary Service handed over food parcels. Churches offered support, both practical and pastoral (one of the men married a church volunteer he met in the shelter). And the Ministry of Labour and the Colonial Office made sure nobody slipped through the net. As one of the men, John Richards, described it: 'There was quite a few of us down there . . . But it wasn't bad. The things were clean and we got food to eat down there, and things like that. But then gradually we dispersed, because some of them, the Army come down and recruit some, the RAF come down and recruit some, everybody got different places. The coal mines, people come down and recruit some at the time, things like that. And they are spread several ways, several places.'[12] The men were processed through the Coldharbour Lane Labour Exchange. Soon, they began what they came over for: 'Within days some started working and within one month all got jobs and left the shelter. And because they worked very hard in the factory or office or whatever it is, all of our people had employment.'[13]

There was a parallel development at the time which puts the men's arrival in a wider context. The independence of India in 1947 and the subsequent Nationality Act in 1948 created two types of British citizen: those of the United Kingdom and Colonies and those of Commonwealth countries. The former were presumed already to have equal status across the Empire; the latter were given the same rights through the Act. Driven by Indian independence, the

Act was designed to enshrine in law equal rights for Commonwealth citizens. Less than two weeks after the *Windrush* docked, the Home Secretary, Chuter Ede, said:

> I know there are also some who feel it is wrong to have a citizenship of the United Kingdom and Colonies. Some people feel it would be a bad thing to give the coloured races of the Empire the idea that, in some way or the other, they are the equals of people in this country. The government do not subscribe to that view. We believe wholeheartedly that the common citizenship of the United Kingdom and Colonies is an essential part of the development of the relationship between this Mother Country and the Colonies.[14]

But for all that, in the medium and long term the Act had a very different impact. It divided British citizens, for the first time, into different categories, a divide which was to have a profound effect in coming decades as Commonwealth immigration began to take off. As Mike and Trevor Phillips put it: '[T]he debate on the Nationality Act was actually the beginning of a trauma about citizenship, race and nationality which swiftly became associated with the arrival of Caribbean immigrants.'[15]

The implications were debated in Cabinet by the next government. On 3 February 1954, under the agenda item 'Coloured Workers', Churchill is quoted, with abbreviations by Cabinet Secretary Sir Norman Brook, as saying: 'Problems wh. will arise if many coloured people settle here. Are we to saddle ourselves with colour problems in UK? Attracted by Welfare State. Public opinion in UK

won't tolerate it once it gets beyond certain limits.'
Florence Horsbrugh, the Minister of Education and MP
for Manchester Moss Side, is recorded as adding: 'Already
becoming serious in Manchr.' Then David Maxwell Fyfe,
the Home Secretary, gave a figure of 40,000 compared to
7000 before the Second World War and raised the possibility of immigration control. He said:

> There is a case on merits for excludg. riff-raff. But polit-
> ically it wd. be represented & discussed on basis of
> colour limitation. That wd. offend the floating vote viz.,
> the old Liberals. We shd. be reversing age-long
> trad[ition] tht. B[ritish] S[ubjects] have right of entry
> to mother-country of Empire. We shd. offend Liberals,
> also sentimentalists . . . The col[onial] pop[ulations] are
> resented in L[iverpool], Paddington & other areas by
> those who come into contact with them. But those who
> don't are apt to take a more Liberal view.

Churchill concluded: 'Ques. is wtr. it is politically wise to
allow public feeling to develop a little more before takg.
action.' It would, he said, be 'fatal' to let the situation
develop too far: 'Wd. lke. also to study possibility of
"quota" – no. not to be exceeded.'[16]

The *Empire Windrush* immigrants were more than symbolic.
Their presence changed Britain, and for the better. There
had long been a black presence in Britain, and other immigrants had also been welcomed before on a much larger
scale than the response to the *Windrush*'s arrival seemed to
suggest. But, small as the actual number of passengers on the

Empire Windrush was, they were the beginning of a wave of immigration unprecedented in scale.

Previous immigrants to Britain had included the 50,000 Huguenots who were admitted in 1572 and 1685, following the St Bartholomew's Day Massacre in Paris and the Revocation of the Edict of Nantes. In the nineteenth century, a small number of Jews fleeing pogroms were allowed in; and in the 1930s, 70,000 refugees from the Nazis were admitted. In 1939 there were 239,000 adult immigrants in the UK (of whom 80,000 were refugees). By 1950 there were 424,329.[17] Of these extra 200,000 the biggest group was 130,000 Poles, of whom 100,000 had served in the Polish armed forces. The rest were refugees who, understandably, did not want to return to their home countries because, after Yalta, they had become Soviet satellites.

They were greeted with a mixture of curiosity and concern, along with widespread press coverage and associated political debates. But as the economy recovered and the need for more workers grew, so it became ever more usual for new arrivals to disembark from passenger ships and, later, planes from the Caribbean – and then not just the Caribbean but also the wider Commonwealth. Not for over 1000 years, since the Norman Conquest, had anything on the scale of the immigration which began in 1948 been contemplated, let alone begun.

The facts of that immigration are clear – although the interpretation placed on them has provoked one of the most profound political and social debates of the past half-century. Until the 1950s, immigration into Britain (other than from Ireland) was piecemeal and had almost no

impact on society overall. But after the *Windrush* generation of immigration had begun, the level ran at around half
a million legal immigrants every decade. This was bound to
have a major impact. In a matter of years, the white, mono-
cultural, settled habits of the population metamorphosed
into the multicultural, multiracial Britain of today. By 1961
there were 250,000 Afro-Caribbeans in the UK, by 1965
400,000, and by 1971 over half a million. Of those from
the Indian subcontinent, the first large group to arrive was
Punjabi Sikhs from the Jullundur Doab, followed by Hindu
Gujaratis from Surat on the north coast of Bombay
(Mumbai). Next were Muslim Mirpuris and Cambellpuris
from north-east Pakistan. Finally came the Muslim Bengalis
from Sylhet. But for all the impact on society of this influx,
initially it had little impact on overall population numbers
as immigration was balanced by a similar level of emigration. What changed was not the absolute population
number but the complexion of that population.

Until, that is, the past two decades. Since the 1990s the
net inflow – from outside the EU – has been 1.5 million a
decade. Today, immigration makes up 83 per cent of population growth.[18] These extracts from recent Office of
National Statistics bulletins show the extent of the change:
'In 2001, 4.9 million (8.3 per cent) of the total population
of the UK [were] born overseas . . . more than double the
2.1 million (4.2 per cent) in 1951[19] . . . In the year to mid-
2005, the UK population increased by 375,000 . . . the
largest annual rise in numbers since 1962 . . . Natural
change (the difference between births and deaths) contributed one third of the population increase. Net migration
and other changes contributed the other two thirds.'[20]

Indeed, one in four children born in Britain now has a foreign parent, compared with one in five in 2001.[21]

So why the change? The lifting of the Iron Curtain in 1989 led to a demographic earthquake, with the break-up of Yugoslavia, war in the Balkans and conflicts in Africa providing notable migration flashpoints. Almost overnight there was a dramatic increase in the number of refugees and asylum seekers. In the 1980s there were no more than 4000 a year.[22] By 2002 there were 84,000. Many were genuine. Many, however, were economic migrants seeking a better life, either through their own efforts or through Britain's generous welfare state. But asylum seekers have never made up the majority of immigrants (although for a few years they were the largest single group). As we have seen with the *Windrush* passengers, the mythology surrounding immigration is rarely correct, however entrenched the apparent certainties may be. For a start, the UK has far more immigrants from the EU than it does from India, Bangladesh, Sri Lanka, Pakistan, the Caribbean and the Middle East combined. But the difference is that it is balanced: roughly the same number leave Britain to move to Europe. With India, Bangladesh, Sri Lanka, Pakistan, the Caribbean, the Middle East and Africa, the immigration is almost totally one-sided.

The four legitimate means of entering the UK are for family reunion and marriage, to study, with a work permit and through EU citizenship. Net (legal) migration has averaged 166,000 a year since 2000. On current trends, immigration will add more than 2 million people every 10 years. The Government Actuary Service estimates that with immigration of 195,000 a year (very close to the present level of legal immigration), the UK population will grow from 59.8 million in 2000 to 68 million in 2031. Part of the reason the birth rate has lifted to a 26-year high (births in 2006 increased for the fifth successive year, to 734,000, compared with 663,000 in 2002) has been the surge in immigration.[23] The highest birth rates are in the overwhelmingly Muslim Pakistani and Bangladeshi communities. The birth rate among women born in Pakistan but living in the UK is three times higher than that among British-born women. The fertility rate (the average number of children a woman has) is now 1.87, up from 1.63 in 2002, which was below the 'replacement rate' necessary to maintain the population (without immigration).[24] The Pakistani rate of 4.7 children per mother is almost three times the British-born rate, while the average immigrant rate is 2.5.

On present trends, around 6 million of the 8 million increase in population will move to London and the southeast. For all the problems which immigration on the pre-1980s scale caused – the Notting Hill and Brixton riots were the most obvious example of racial tensions – the sheer scale of these increases is of a different order from anything that has gone before and it is difficult to predict with certainty what impact this will have. There is a lazy assumption that it must, of necessity, cause deep-seated and irreversible friction. But it need not necessarily be this way.

When an issue appears to be at its most intractable, it almost always pays dividends to turn to the writings of Milton Friedman. Professor Friedman, as was his habit, summed up the real issue in ten words: 'You cannot simultaneously have free immigration and a welfare state.' If the opportunity exists to move from an area paying negligible benefits to one paying relatively lavish benefits, then the decision to go to where the benefits are higher is what is best termed a 'no brainer'. But sensible debate on immigration has become impossible because we confuse those who want to work – those who move in order to better themselves – with those who merely want to take advantage of better benefits; and we damn both groups equally. By far the most corrosive cause of bad race relations is the immigrant who lives off the state. The main lesson from the rise of extremist fringe parties in Europe and the growing success of the British National Party (BNP) in garnering support in areas with large immigrant populations is that if mainstream parties ignore the issues that the electorate thinks matter, voters either stay away from the polls altogether or turn to the parties which do talk about them.

The British are, by their nature, a tolerant people. We have a proud tradition of giving a welcome to those who want to better their lot. My own ancestors did just that at the end of the nineteenth century. They came here to escape the pogroms and to work, and were fiercely proud that, having arrived with nothing, they built themselves good lives through their own efforts. That is the British tradition. And we should be similarly welcoming to their successors, new immigrants who are similarly committed to a new life and who want to better themselves through hard work. We will all benefit from their industry and enterprise. Icons of British life such as fish and chips, the Mini and Marks & Spencer all emanate from immigrants to the UK. Such enterprise and hard work have long been the engines which have driven the US to its astonishing wealth and prosperity.

But there is a fundamental contradiction between this approach and the benefits culture which has taken hold in the UK, which means that unproductive immigrants who come here in order to live off the state have poisoned the well even for those whom we should welcome.

Economics and rationality tend to fly out of the window when confronted with immigration. It is almost impossible to talk about the benefits of immigration without being regarded as hopelessly liberal and naive. In the early 1990s, the British government refused to grant visas to the Hong Kong Chinese almost entirely because of the political calculation that the public would not stomach another mass influx of immigrants. Yet that was, on any calculation, a major economic blunder. Vancouver, which welcomed 230,000 people from Hong Kong between 1991 and 1996, has reaped the rewards ever since. It is the British economy which lost out, not the migrants.

In this context, the Danish election of 2001 was fascinating. The political climate there was much like that in Britain, in that there was a deep and growing fear of immigration. The centre-right Liberal Party focused on immigration as the main election issue. But instead of the usual anti-immigration rhetoric, it turned on its head the main concern of electors, that immigrants are somehow a leech on the state, and in doing so won an unexpected victory. Denmark, it said, should welcome immigrants. But for their first seven years they should receive no state benefits of any kind, other than schooling for their children and emergency health care. And that, more or less, was that. Such an approach squared the immigration circle. It permitted the gains which immigrants can bring to a country; it dealt with the problem of benefit leeches (as the party leader and Prime Minister, Anders Fogh Rasmussen, put it during the Danish election campaign: 'Denmark must not be the social security office for the rest of the world'); and it neutralized the far right's racist arguments. Since immigrants could only prosper through their own efforts and the economy would prosper with them, there would be no rational reason not to welcome them.

The benefits of such an approach are more than economic. As the US experience shows, the greater the premium placed on work, the easier it is for immigrants to assimilate and be accepted. Every American generation believes that in the past immigration was good, while now it is bad. But the same patterns repeat themselves. The evidence suggests that the quality of people migrating to the US (measured by the standard of completed education) has continued to improve as, for example, Mexico's school system has expanded. The key is work and economic integration. In the US, a quarter of immigrants have less than 9 years of schooling and start in poor jobs. The US is a middle-class country importing a working class, but after 10 to 15 years in the US the average immigrant earns more than the average US-born worker. Within 20 years, 60 per cent of immigrants become home-owners; indeed, within 25 years they are more likely to own their home than native-born Americans. And the second generation is a greater success still, an upward mobility prompted by education. Immigrants' children drop out of school a full third less than US-born children, and do an average of 2 hours' homework a day compared to the US-born average of 30 minutes.

Why has the US been so much better at integrating such a large number of immigrants? Tamar Jacoby, one of the leading US analysts, points to a number of key factors. First, the US has been at it a long time compared with Britain. There are no 'hereditary Americans'; you simply 'show up and participate'. There is no single strongly established religion and thus less sense of outsiderdom and otherness. Latinos have a long tradition of mixing, compared with Muslims. Crime is not a particular problem amongst US immigrants and so there is less negative stereotyping. And the US labour market is far more flexible, its welfare state less important, than in the UK.

The lesson to draw from this is that immigration policy should be based on work, with welfare assistance only as humanitarian aid where necessary. The greater the premium on work, the easier it is to assimilate and be accepted. The welfare state is something of a curse, discouraging work and assimilation. Laws which prevent immigrants working and force them underground are counterproductive, hindering assimilation and criminalizing otherwise useful immigrants.

Dislike of immigrants is based on more than their being a drain; it is also that their 'otherness' poses a threat to the solidity of national culture. Too much government assistance is thus a problem even for the immigrants themselves. Welfare discourages work and, as a result, the assimilation which is essential for the long-term health of the host country.

The problem with current discussions of the subject is that the word 'immigration' serves no useful purpose on its own, since wrapped up in it are two wholly different concepts – the productive and the unproductive immigrant – to which our approach should be very different. If immigrants are committed to a new life and want to better themselves, wonderful: we will all benefit from their industry. But if they want simply to take advantage of a better reward for doing nothing, there is no reason – moral, practical or legal – why we need to give them anything, least of all an open house.

2

THE ARTS

9 August 1946

On 9 August 1946, the Arts Council received its Royal Charter, and with that the 'Robin-Hood-in-reverse' principle of culture began. From then on, taxpayers' money was to be used to finance the tastes of a small minority of the public, with the perverse consequence (perverse, given that it was the opposite of what was intended) that high culture became even less accessible to the wider public. Paid to write for a small audience, that is exactly what those artists did.

Arts subsidy on the modern model of tax funding, rather than the traditional philanthropic model, began long before the formal granting of a Royal Charter to the Arts Council. In the late nineteenth century, public funds were allocated to the purchase of paintings and the maintenance of museums such as the Victoria and Albert. And the Arts

Council itself emerged from the Committee for the Encouragement of Music and the Arts (CEMA, as it was known) which began life on 9 January 1940 with a gift of £300 to the National Federation of Women's Institutes to pay for the salary of an 'adviser/organizer' for music.

CEMA was set up at the start of the Second World War with the aim of promoting and maintaining British culture. Its origins lay in the Pilgrim Trust, a charity started in 1930 by Edward Harkness, an Anglophile American philanthropist whose money came from his father's holdings in Standard Oil. The Pilgrim Trust was set up with an endowment from Harkness of over £2 million, 'prompted by his admiration for what Great Britain had done in the 1914–18 war' as the Trust Deed put it, 'and by his ties of affection for the land from which he drew his descent'. The gift was intended to be used 'to give grants for some of the country's more urgent needs and in promoting her future well-being'.

At the start of the war in 1939, the government reconstituted the Entertainments National Service Association (ENSA), which had worked during the First World War to entertain the troops. But ministers soon started to think that a civilian counterpart might be necessary to preserve 'the national framework of culture, with special reference to music, drama and the arts', as a Board of Education memo had it.[1] But in typical Whitehall fashion, even after the idea had been approved in theory, discussions plodded on to no effect. It was private bodies that stepped forward with practical ideas, culminating in the Pilgrim Trust's establishment of CEMA.

In October 1939, the Director of the National Gallery,

Sir Kenneth Clark, established a series of lunchtime concerts at the gallery; such was their success that he decided to launch a larger-scale project. He asked Thomas Jones (known as 'T.J.'), the Secretary of the Pilgrim Trust and a former civil servant on first-name terms with the likes of Stanley Baldwin, Lloyd George and Lord Astor, to join him in the project. At the same time, officials from the Board of Education and the Treasury also made contact with the Trust as a possible funder and administrator for their own idea of a civilian version of ENSA. Earl De La Warr, the President of the Board of Education (precursor to the modern office of Education Secretary), wrote to T.J. that the National Gallery concerts demonstrated 'an almost pathetic hunger for such provision'.[2]

De La Warr was an honourable man. He had been brought into the Cabinet by Neville Chamberlain as Lord Privy Seal but came to disagree with appeasement and, in Cabinet, argued that Britain should go to war to 'free the world from the constant threat of ultimatums'. For this, he was demoted in October 1938 to the post of President of the Board of Education. De La Warr did not think it appropriate that such provision should be publicly funded, first because the real need was to support amateurs: 'those who are making music and acting plays for themselves, because I realise all that this means to their own morale'; and second because not only would tax funding 'be very difficult to get', it would also stifle creativity – a prescient reservation given the history which this chapter relates. So he asked the Pilgrim Trust to provide £25,000 to fund the plan. His idea was, he admitted, makeshift; longer term, the Treasury was interested 'in principle' in providing funding.

And, he added, after the war he would like the Board of Education to maintain its interest in culture.

The Pilgrim Trust responded with the idea of sending musicians across the country to organize choirs, concerts and other amateur musical performances. It went down well with De La Warr and on 19 December the Pilgrim Trust formally set up its Committee for the Encouragement of Music and the Arts, funded and staffed by its own people but with offices inside the Board of Education. The Committee itself comprised Lord Macmillan, the chairman of the Pilgrim Trust, T.J., Sir Kenneth Clark, Sir Walford Davies, who had pioneered the broadcasting of music, Thelma Cazalet MP and W.E. Williams, Director of the British Institute of Adult Education and, appropriately, originator of the Institute's Art for the People touring exhibitions. The Committee made its first grants on 9 January 1940 and appointed a secretary, Mary Glasgow, a junior civil servant at the Board. Mary Glasgow was to remain a linchpin of arts subsidy for the next twelve years, as the secretary general of CEMA and then of the new Arts Council.

CEMA's focus on supporting amateur performance was not universally lauded. The economist John Maynard Keynes, who considered himself an aesthete and a man of the highest taste, doted on artists: he married a ballerina and conducted affairs with male artists. He believed that the role of subsidy ought primarily to be the raising of performance standards, which necessarily implied professional and focused performances. That split – between the spreading of art for art's sake and the inculcation of elite standards – has remained at the heart of the debate surrounding arts funding ever since. CEMA soon abandoned its policy of funding only amateur performances. Sir George Dyson, a composer and the Director of the Royal College of Music, agreed to take charge of twenty concerts by the London Philharmonic and London Symphony Orchestras, to be bankrolled by CEMA and put on in industrial areas within fifty miles of London.

There is almost no example in human history of a body such as CEMA sticking to its initial remit; it is in the very DNA of committees to seek to expand their role. And, sure enough, within a matter of months CEMA decided to apply to the Treasury for money – a matching £25,000 – to pay for the funding of professional performances, which would be far more to the taste of the grandees on the Committee. The money was handed over. (Such people are rarely backward in expecting the state to pay for their pleasures. And their successors would come up with another wheeze by which their tastes could be funded by the rest of society: the National Lottery.)

With Treasury funding came reorganization: the committee was to be appointed by the Board of Education and wholly state-funded. Another lesson of history is that when the state starts to fund activities previously funded by private money, the private money dries up. The Pilgrim Trust had given another £12,500 in January 1941 and a further £12,500 in March 1942, making a total of £50,000. But as CEMA sought and received state funding, the Trust saw no reason to continue its support. With its departure, so too its chairman, Macmillan, and the Trust secretary, T.J., left the Committee. The new-look CEMA had a budget of £100,000. It began by offering a £6000 guarantee for an Old Vic tour of *Macbeth* to Wales. Its concerts – in marked and often remarked-upon contrast to ENSA's activities – were decidedly highbrow. This was a product of the change in direction under the new chairman, Keynes, who took over on 1 April 1942. Keynes had been reluctant to accept the position but soon realized that he had the opportunity to shape the nation's cultural life – a chance he could not resist. He wrote to his colleagues that CEMA should be focused on 'the greatest works of dramatic, musical and pictorial art, with the most accomplished actors, performers and productions, with the national orchestras, and with the national art collections'.[3] He got to work immediately, announcing at his first Committee meeting that opera and ballet should fall within CEMA's remit as well as the de facto national theatre and opera, the Old Vic–Sadler's Wells axis. Next would come classical music, with revenue guarantees for orchestras. He added the thought that, in time, artists working in organizations supported by the state should become salaried, pensionable state employees, treated in much the same way as civil servants. It was, of course, pure coincidence that the overwhelming proportion of the subsidy went to those bodies with which Keynes was already associated and enjoyed visiting in London.

It wasn't just CEMA's priorities and plans that Keynes changed: in February 1943 he complained about its 'dreadful name', not least because acronyms were 'undignified' and – heavens! – 'something too much like ENSA for our taste'. His favoured name was the Royal Council for the Arts.[4] After much bureaucratic debate, the name 'Arts Council of Great Britain' was agreed, with an initial £235,000 annual funding. In August 1946 the King granted the Arts Council a Royal Charter, and in doing so formally destroyed any chance of high culture seeking to broaden rather than narrow its reach: the precise opposite of the stated aim of the Arts Council.

The phrase 'dumbing down' is over-used and somewhat misleading. There is nothing wrong with providing entertainment that does not require the brain to engage. We all need to switch off sometimes. If people are prepared to pay their own money for something, it can be as dumb as they want it to be.

The problem with today's cultural life lies not in the private sector, where the accusation of dumbing down is usually made, but rather with subsidy. Subsidy has some merit if it makes high culture available to all, either by reducing the cost of admission or by making possible an art form which might otherwise have been prohibitively expensive (such as opera). But that original intention has been lost – indeed, it barely ever existed – with tax subsidy today little more than a transfer of money from the poor to a tiny cultural elite who use it to pay for their own esoteric pleasures.

According to the British Federation of Festivals, over 300 festivals take place every year, from Lichfield, Larmer Tree and Cheltenham to York, Cambridge, Harrogate and Fishguard. It sounds wonderful – spreading culture and pleasure across the nation. The reality is rather different. Take the Huddersfield Festival. A recent programme featured the composer Helmut Oehring. As the brochure puts it: 'His parents were deaf mutes and a lot of his music explores the relationship between music and deaf people.' The truth of the matter is that most of these festivals are not so much a waste of time as a waste of money – my money and yours. They do, of course, give pleasure to their audiences (although it is unclear what state one has to be in to enjoy 'Folk at the Fish – Fishguard Arms, Haverfordwest. Folk music and song from the landlord himself', part of a recent Fishguard Festival). But do not fall for the idea beloved of the arts world that the network of tax-subsidized festivals is just a more professional re-creation of traditional British celebrations of local arts and crafts, institutions which sprang up quite naturally to fill the leisure time granted in the wake of the 1847 Factory Act, which limited the working day to ten hours. They are not. They are part of one of the most lavishly financed, most exclusive, most iniquitous and most self-satisfied industries in the country: the money pit known as 'the arts'. The summer festival season, for example, highlights the perversion of the original idea of festivals. The first recorded 'festival' was the Workington Festival in Cumberland in 1869, where the entertainment comprised a band and a choir. During the First World War, evacuees who were at school for only half a day were offered lessons in dance, poetry, painting and music in their spare time and festivals were created for them to show off their new skills. Today, almost all trace of that genuine community purpose has disappeared and they are merely a further example of the arts establishment spending other people's money on its own minority tastes.

There are few clearer examples of the Robin-Hood-in-reverse principle than the recent explosion in such arts festivals. The entire racket is run by administrators who glide seamlessly from one public-sector job to another, using taxpayers' money to finance their own minority tastes and then taking the high moral ground when it is put to them that they are engaged in a form of grand larceny: obtaining money from those who have no interest in any of their efforts and using it to fund retrospectives of the paintings of Lucian Freud and 'artist in profile' concerts exploring the work of Karlheinz Stockhausen, to take just two recent examples.

Arts Council England spent £1.1 billion of public money between 2006 and 2008. And how elevating it is to discover where that money is going: a fourfold grant increase, for instance, to the Luton Carnival, to a total of £124,500. Luton wouldn't be Luton without its carnival, after all, and which of us is not thrilled to have worked that extra hour to pay more tax to help fund it? £220,000 was given to The Drum arts project in Birmingham – a 65 per cent rise; £90,000 to Kala Sangam, a multicultural arts project in Bradford – a 150 per cent rise; and £51,000 was handed over to the 'craft organisation', Shisha. In 2004, Arts Council England provided an 'investment' of £3.5 million in 'decibel', a 'one-off initiative to raise the profile of culturally diverse arts in England'. 'Street artists' ('buskers' is, it seems, a derogatory term) are also well looked after: Zap in Brighton received £25,000; Circus Space has been given £70,000 a year and Circomedia is funded to the tune of £80,000 to train 'artists' who will perform on the streets. One might have been under the impression that buskers got their money from passers-by, depending on whether or not they were any good. It is, of course, much more sensible to take money from taxpayers and hand it over to mime artists to make sure they are always in pocket. How philistine we would be as a society if the Covent Garden Piazza were not properly staffed with fire-eaters.

The real problem is that arts funding is a monster which, once given its head, develops an insatiable appetite and spends, almost literally, for spending's sake. As Arts Council England's 'Manifesto' expresses it: 'In 2002's spending round, we achieved a major increase in public investment in the arts. Now we intend to capitalise on that success by backing the country's artistic talent and winning further support for the arts.' In other words: if you think we were whooping it up at your expense before, that was nothing. ('Manifesto' is an interesting label, given that the Arts Council is a body which is set up specifically to ignore the public's wishes and provide an income to organizations that they would not receive through the free choices made by consumers in the market.)

Rarely is the money spent as the public – who supply it – would choose to spend it. Nothing better illustrates this than the National Lottery fiasco. More than £500 million has gone on building new museums and extensions since the first tranche of lottery funding became available in 1995. Instead of using the money to help existing museums, with proven track records of providing services which the public used, it was instead frittered away on a series of follies, the upkeep of which alone added another £29 million a year to the running costs of the country's museums. Kevin Costner might have become a hero to a generation for believing, in the film *Field of Dreams*, that 'if you build it, they will come', but his character was using his own money. The lesson of lottery funding is: if the arts establishment decides to build it, they won't come. The Life

Force Centre, built beside Bradford Cathedral at a cost of £5 million, closed in 2001 after seven months. It was projected to attract 40,000 people a year; in its first week it had 62 paying visitors. The Centre for Visual Arts in Cardiff was forecast to have 220,000 visitors in its first year. It managed 47,500 and closed in November 2001 after costing £9 million to build. The £15-million National Centre for Popular Music in Sheffield closed after 16 months in 2000. It was supposed to attract 400,000 people a year. Fewer than 90,000 went through its doors. On and on it goes.

The National Lottery is in fact the most blatant example of the 'Robin-Hood-in-reverse' scam in the UK. And such was its clear, explicit purpose from the very beginning. The founder of the lottery was Lord (Victor) Rothschild, chairman of the Royal Commission on Gambling in the late 1970s, which recommended 'a national lottery for good causes'. It would have three characteristics: it would be a national monopoly, offering unlimited prize money so as to maximize revenue; its proceeds would go to the arts, sport and 'other deserving causes'; and it was to operate autonomously of the Treasury. As Lord Rothschild put it in the report: 'There is a crucial need in our society for a source of substantial funds to provide support of a kind with which any government experiences great difficulty. The objective should not be to replace the function of central government but rather to fill the gap created by the inevitable disappearance, in a society where the accumulation of private wealth has become much more difficult, of private support of worthy causes on a large scale.'[5] In other words, there are too few private philanthropists; governments do the bidding of ordinary voters; and a way has to be found to get someone to pay for those aspects of culture valued by the great and the good. So lure the philistine ordinary folk in to do just that, with the chance of untold wealth. As for letting the people who fund the lottery have a say in how its money is spent: ugh! In typically patrician fashion, that was dealt with by the vague phrase 'other deserving causes' and the inclusion of sport as a safety valve to make the process more acceptable.

That safety valve was used to great political effect by the first Secretary of State for National Heritage, David Mellor, who was responsible for the initial stages of the lottery in 1992. He may only have lasted five months in the job – the (false) allegation of his love-making in a Chelsea shirt and other amorous adventures put paid to his political career – but that was all the time he needed to take the key decision required to hoodwink the oiks into paying for his personal artistic pleasures; he was, and remains, a fanatical opera and classical music fan. He defined five 'good causes': the arts, national heritage, the Millennium Fund, sport and chari-ties. Crucially, he decreed that they should receive equal shares of the pot of money made available from the lottery revenue. This meant that arts and culture would take two thirds of the money, but including sport and charity as good causes meant that money was available to almost every conceivable activity which the public would want funded. And just as expected, when the lottery was launched charities were almost always cited first among the good causes which would benefit. Indeed, opinion polls conducted after the launch showed that lottery players thought that charities were the prime beneficiaries from the lottery. In fact, however, charities complained bitterly that their income fell, since previous donors thought they no longer needed to give so generously, as the lottery was taking care of the charities' revenue.

This came as no surprise to those responsible for the lottery. As David Mellor himself put it in the Commons debate on the National Lottery Bill in 1995, when he was a backbencher: 'It was never part of the original thinking of the lottery that charities would be beneficiaries.' They had been included to provide 'compensation for any losses'. And – giving the game away – 'nothing could be worse than debates in this place being disfigured by people saying that charities were going to lose out and so we could not have a national lottery'. The lottery had to carry 'credibility with the public, most of whom would not put money into the collecting tins of the organizations that have benefited'.[6] Of course not: so extort the money from them with dreams of wealth.

And, as Rothschild recommended, it has from the start been left to the great and the good to spend the money. There is not even any special accountability for the spending of this largesse. The money is simply doled out to the existing quangos of the arts establishment – heritage money to the National Heritage Memorial Fund (originally chaired by Lord (Jacob) Rothschild) and arts funding to the Arts Council. The Millennium Fund was new but overseen by an assemblage of the usual arts establishment suspects. Today, the revenue is divided between the Big Lottery Fund, which funds charities, health, education, environmental and millennium projects; the Arts Councils; the Sports Councils; and the Heritage Lottery Fund.

It has all worked a treat. The Department of National

Heritage's working assumption was that after three years there would be £1.5 to £2.5 billion in revenue. By the end of the first year sales were at £4.3 billion. In 1991, two thirds of adults gambled on the lottery. By 1995 it was 91 per cent.[7] Camelot, the administrators of the lottery, argued in its first year that it was a truly classless institution: 'There isn't one socio-economic group playing at the expense of any other.'[8] This was about as far from the truth as it is possible to get. It is true that all classes play. But the evidence shows that, in terms of both numbers playing and amounts gambled, the lottery depends disproportionately on the poor. Right from the start, Camelot's own data showed the proportion of ABs playing was far lower than for Cs, Ds and Es. In 2005 only 21.1 per cent of ABs played, whilst 28.8 per cent of C2s and 27 per cent of Ds played. The absolute spending figures are even more striking. In 2005 the average weekly bet in households from social group C2 (skilled manual workers) was £2.61, and in social groups D and E £2.32 – 17p more than the average weekly bet from households in social groups A and B.[9] Thanks to the National Lottery, the poor are, quite literally, paying for the pleasures of the wealthy.

Worse even than that, the wealthy have simply used the National Lottery to get cash. The very first grant made by the National Heritage Memorial Fund was £13 million to the Churchill family to buy Winston Churchill's papers. On and on it went, buying up paintings from the already vastly wealthy. As one anonymous member of the Fund put it: 'We could hardly do otherwise. Picassos, Dalis and Magrittes do tend to belong to rich people.'[10] Quite. But that was the very point of the lottery: finding a means to get the poor to hand money over to the rich. Such direct transfers of money – such as the Arts Council's first lottery grant, which handed £55 million to the Royal Opera House – were simply more explicit than the usual subsidy.

There might perhaps be some justification for this if it really did open up new experiences; if it broadened the take-up of high culture and gave people what they wanted but couldn't afford, or didn't even realize they wanted. But it has done none of that. Even if we ignore the inherent cynicism of the wealthy getting everyone else to subsidize their cultural tastes, subsidy has had another wholly damaging effect. It has made culture not more but less accessible. Take music, which provides the most telling example of this.

Any averagely culturally aware person is au fait with the latest fiction, films and theatre. As for new music, however – modern classical rather than pop or rock – forget it. They might have heard of Birtwistle and Boulez, but only through the occasional feature in the newspapers. The chance of them having heard any of their music is close to zero. Modern classical music is a cult pursuit amongst a tiny proportion of the already small minority who are interested in high culture.

The cause of this is not, as some would have it, mysterious. There is no puzzle as to why so few people are even aware of the premiere of a piece of music, let alone interested in going to hear it. The reason is straightforward. Modern classical music took a wrong turn in the 1950s and 1960s. Composers stopped writing for their public and wrote instead for a small clique, because not only were they freed from any obligation to secure an audience for their music, they were also pilloried and starved of funds if that was their aim.

Twentieth-century music is often lumped together and dismissed as unlistenable to by those people who now reject modern classical music. The blame for this wrong turn in music is often attributed to Schoenberg and his twelve-tone scale, which alienated audiences and regarded melody as a crime. Schoenberg, it is often said, destroyed the audience for modern classical music. But this is quite wrong. There were many classical composers who were still able to engage with mass audiences: Britten, Vaughan Williams and Tippett, to name just three. The ruination of classical music as part of mainstream culture came not because of musicians but because of subsidy. Or, to be more specific, because of the BBC, and the deleterious impact of one man's control of musical subsidy. That man was Sir William Glock, who stands responsible for the death of classical music as a generalized cultural pursuit.

A former Controller of the BBC Third Programme (the forerunner of Radio 3), Sir William might be thought an obscure figure of no importance outside the small world of Third Programme listeners. On the contrary, he was in large measure responsible for ruining mass culture. Glock spent thirteen years, from 1959 to 1972, in the post. In that time, he operated an effective blacklist of popular composers – anyone who wrote tonal music with tunes, which had for centuries been the bedrock of classical music – and replaced them with the likes of Boulez, Berio, Nono, Dallapiccola, Carter, Gerhard, Stockhausen and Ligeti, whose tuneless, atonal music almost set out to drive audiences away as a badge of success. His policy instigated a vicious circle: because almost no tonal music would be commissioned by the BBC – then by far the most influential arts organization in the country – composers (who react to incentives like everyone else) turned their back on tunes and started to compose to Glock's, rather than the public's, taste. This in turn meant that classical music was forced to rely on subsidy, since audiences would not pay to listen to it. Where, before, the informed middle classes would have been as informed about the latest classical music as they were about the latest painting or novel, in the new Glockian world classical music became the preserve of a tiny number of obsessives. This led to a chasm between popular and classical music, a chasm which exists to this day.

Simon Heffer, the biographer of Vaughan Williams, has also written about the almost entirely forgotten British composer George Lloyd, one of those on Glock's blacklist:

> Born in 1913, he was such a prodigy that he had two operas put on at Covent Garden before the war. In 1939, when certain composers fled from having to engage the Nazi threat, he joined the Royal Marines, and was in the engine room of HMS *Trinidad* when she was hit by one of her own faulty torpedoes on the Arctic convoys in 1942. His wife was told he was so shell-shocked he would never live again outside an institution. She decided to prove his doctors wrong, and did. By 1945, he was writing music again, at first for only 10 minutes a day, such were the noises in his head. But he just got on with it, and within a year had written his

masterpiece, the hour-long Fourth Symphony. However, no one would perform it. In the new Britain of the Arts Council, and of Leftist bureaucrats and their creatures deciding what the public would be offered by way of art, and who would be bribed with state funds to provide it, George didn't stand a chance. He wrote romantic music in the vein of Verdi, whom he described as his 'god'. That, coupled with his entrepreneurial views, did for him. For more than 20 years, he retreated to Dorset. Instead of whining that the state owed him, as an artist, a living, he made a fortune growing mushrooms and carnations near Sherborne. He continued to write music in his spare time: the final toll, when he died aged 85, was 12 symphonies, four piano concertos, three operas, various choral works, and piles of smaller pieces for everything from piano to brass band. Eventually, a prominent admirer – the pianist John Ogdon – sneaked the score of his eighth symphony into Radio Three which, years after having blacklisted him for his failure to 'conform', actually played it. His Sixth Symphony was put on at the Proms. And quite by accident, in 1981, I heard on the wireless the first performance – 35 years after its completion – of his Fourth Symphony, an event from which I still feel in a state of shock after nearly three decades. An American tycoon heard his music, paid to have it recorded and sent Lloyd, in his seventies, around the world to conduct it . . . He would tell me how he would attend meetings of the Society of Composers and sit aghast as profoundly untalented people sat around complaining about the lack of state funding for their 'jobs'. Lloyd, who had hardly ever received a penny in public subsidy in his life, could not grasp this mentality . . . [Lloyd] always argued that if the state paid composers to write what they liked, they would write self-indulgent rubbish. It has to be said that the weight of empirical evidence is on his side in this argument.[11]

Glock may have given up his control of the purse strings in 1972 but the impact of his wrecking remains. It is only now that there is the odd sprinkling of hope, as composers such as James MacMillan and Thomas Adès set a path which is fully modern but also accessible, that a new generation of composers can start to compose for audiences rather than in spite of them. MacMillan is as eloquent with words as with music, and in January 2008 he wrote of the rigid mindset which still dominates the arts: 'a cultural regime which adjudicates artists and their work on the basis of how they contribute to the remodelling, indeed the overthrow of society's core institutions and ethics'; the view that 'anything that is not Left-wing is intrinsically and irredeemably evil'.

It is impossible not to deal with politics when examining the history of British elite culture, since those responsible for handing out the subsidy are clear that the recipients must conform to their own political prejudices. MacMillan explained it thus:

This has its roots in Romanticism, of course, but a gradual systemisation of radical politics settled in the early 20th century. Think of how, from the 1920s, groups such as Imagists, Vorticists, Futurists, Surrealists, Expressionists habitually declare their commitment to Revolution. Yes, any old revolution would do, but as long as it overturned manners and lifestyles as well as aesthetics and politics. This has nothing to do with a love of life, a love of the poor or the outsider, but all to do with a love of transgression. It becomes addictive and in the past has led artists as much to the extreme Right as to the far Left. Childish 'anti-bourgeois' militancy has no political intelligence or moral fibre. Witness, for example, Harold Pinter's descent into infantilism every time he mentions the United States, or for that matter decides to write poetry. Rather than being ridiculed for the embarrassing doggerel-merchant he has become, he is lauded to the highest by his fellow-travellers, easily impressed by easy rhetoric and equally determined to maintain their favoured positions in the back-slapping arts establishment. The legacy of this militancy can be seen nowadays in 'arts criticism' and the rise of a secular priesthood whose dogmas we now endure day in, day out. The common purpose of this new cultural élite is to attack the institutions and principles of our shared common life. What passes in Britain for an intelligentsia has appropriated the Arts for their own designs – a recent debate at the South Bank proclaimed 'All Modern Art Is Left Wing'. No dissent from the party line goes unpunished.[12]

As if to prove his point, the response of the artistic director of the Soho Theatre, Lisa Goldman, to being asked why so few plays challenge the left-liberal consensus, demonstrated with unintentional clarity the blinkers which guide the cultural elite: 'What would a right-wing play have to offer?

Anti-democracy, misogyny, bigotry, nostalgia of all kinds? Let's get back to a white Britain? That the slave trade had a civilising influence? That women should stay in the home?'

This prejudice against anything not seen as politically acceptable was on display in 2007, the 150th anniversary of Sir Edward Elgar's birth. That's the same Elgar who is generally viewed as the greatest British composer of the past 250 years. The composer of the finest cello concerto in the repertory, two magisterial symphonies, the *Enigma Variations*, the *Pomp and Circumstance* marches . . . the list of Elgar's immortal pieces goes on. But ask Arts Council England what they think of arguably the greatest British artist of modern times and the answer appears to be: nothing. The Elgar Society asked Arts Council England for £174,000 to organize a series of concerts for young people around the anniversary of Elgar's birth. They were met with a point-blank refusal. Because, of course, arts subsidy is not about enabling performances which the public want to hear. And Elgar, with his mass popularity – and, worse, his unforgivable sin of patriotism – is anathema to the cultural commissars who run the arts subsidy racket. Arts Council England said that the Elgar Society's bid failed to meet any of the criteria by which applications are judged – a glorious piece of circular reasoning which enables them to give £12,000 to an 'artist' in the East Midlands to kick an empty curry box along a street because it meets their criteria, and to refuse to contribute towards concerts which celebrate the life of one of our greatest ever artists.

So while £174,000 for Elgar is a no-no, funding the

Huddersfield Contemporary Music Festival's performances of Helmut Oehring's music exploring 'the relationship between music and deaf people' is a definite yes.

For that, we have the creation of the Arts Council to thank.

3

EDUCATION

12 July 1965

On 12 July 1965, the English state education sector was injected with a dose of poison. The system was far from perfect; there was a long tail of underperforming schools. But on that day, the British government pledged its official commitment to the end of all that was good about state education.

It was not, of course, presented like that. Rather, as the Department of Education and Science put it in Circular 10/65, it was simply complying with a motion passed by the House of Commons on 21 January 1965:

That this House, conscious of the need to raise educational standards at all levels, and regretting that the realisation of this objective is impeded by the separation of children into different types of secondary schools, notes with approval the efforts of local authorities to reorganise secondary education on comprehensive lines which will preserve all that is valuable in grammar school education for those children who now receive it and make it available to more children; recognises that the method and timing of such reorganisation should vary to meet local needs; and believes that the time is now ripe for a declaration of national policy.

And in doing that, Circular 10/65 was issued: 'The Secretary of State accordingly requests local education authorities, if they have not already done so, to prepare and submit to him plans for reorganising secondary education in their areas on comprehensive lines. The purpose of this Circular is to provide some central guidance on the methods by which this can be achieved.'

It might have used the word 'requests'. But in practice, the department used its power not merely to request but to require such a change, refusing to pay for any new school or improvements to existing schools which were not comprehensive. And with that came the end not merely of grammar schools, which had had a transformational impact on the lives of so many poor but bright children, but also of what has come to be known as traditional education, replaced by so-called progressive methodologies which spread the anti-education virus throughout the system.

If it was not so awful it would be hilarious – the idea that the single greatest act of educational vandalism in British history was meant to raise educational standards. For all that there were problems with two legs of the old tripartite system (the technical and secondary modern schools), one wing of British state education, grammar schools, did a fine job of lifting children out of poverty and giving them opportunity. Yet today, our system has one of the worst rankings in the developed world; every opinion poll shows that the majority of parents would pay to escape the state system if they could afford to do so. In June 2008, for example, 57 per cent of parents said that they would send their child to a private school if they could afford it. Of those who said they would prefer a private education for their child, 66 per cent cited 'better standards' and 30 per cent better discipline in private schools.[1]

There was, however, nothing inevitable about this. There is no comparable problem in the rest of Europe, where academic and vocational selection have remained widely practised and state schools have, in the main, succeeded in the task of offering decent opportunities to all children. The responsibility for our failure lies with the comprehensive ideology which gripped first the education establishment and then politicians in the 1960s.

Although the arguments for comprehensive schooling had been floated since the 1950s, they were initially regarded as merely one option – and a decidedly politically partisan one at that. Had Tony Crosland not been Education Secretary, and had he not issued Circular 10/65, education would almost certainly have looked very different today, as this near-compulsory shift to the comprehensive system would not have happened.

The comprehensive revolution had two goals: one educational, the other social. Many of the most influential educational theorists in the 1950s and 1960s genuinely believed that mixed-ability teaching and comprehensive schooling 'give all children a fresh start in the secondary school . . . The expectations which teachers have of the majority of their pupils are better – and their pupils, sensing and responding to this higher regard, in turn achieve more,'[2] as one of the leading advocates, Robin Pedley, put it at the time. There was also a more profound objective underlying the reform. 'In spite of the virtual abolition of poverty, in spite of the rise there has been in the rewards of labour, in spite of the fact that . . . the great bulk of the nation now regards itself as middle class, Britain is still a jealous and divided nation,'[3] argued *The Times* in 1961. Education, which was seen by the advocates of comprehensive schools as 'a serious alternative to nationalisation in promoting a more just and efficient society' (as Tony Crosland, who would not rest until he had 'destroyed every fucking grammar school', to use his infamous phrase, is said to have put it), was thus to be a vital plank in moving towards a classless society. Pedley went on: 'Comprehensive education does more than open the doors of opportunity to all children. It represents a different, a larger and more generous attitude of mind . . . the forging of a communal culture by the pursuit of quality with equality, by the education of their pupils in and for democracy, and by the creation of happy, vigorous, local communities in which the school is the focus of social and educational life.'[4]

It was, of course, Grade A nonsense. Even on its own terms the destruction of the grammar schools – the one undoubted social success of English state education – has failed, making class divisions worse rather than better. As we have seen, those who can, leave the state system for private education or move to a pleasant middle-class catchment area. The rest are stuck with what they are served up. A.H. Halsey, an adviser to Crosland and one of the leading egalitarian theorists of the 1960s, has summarized the position with stark honesty: '[T]he essential fact of twentieth-century educational history is that egalitarian policies have failed.'[5] But what is now obvious – and was obvious to many at the time – was hidden from the blinkered minds of the ideologically driven fundamentalists of the comprehensive revolution, led politically by Anthony Crosland.

In January 1965, Crosland was moved from his role as George Brown's deputy at the Department for Economic Affairs and promoted to the Cabinet, at forty-six its youngest member. He was, according to Brown, 'an exceptionally able administrator', despite a reputation as a thinker rather than a doer, and his old boss was reluctant to lose him.[6] But from day one, Crosland entered the Department of Education and Science (DES) with a focus and determination which belied the doubters. As his biographer writes: 'What impressed civil servants and political colleagues alike was the minister's clarity and sense of purpose. In subsequent ministerial posts, Crosland usually took time to settle in and he believed it required at least six months to get a sound grasp of how a department worked. But at the DES he had already written extensively on the subject before he arrived and felt confident of the issues requiring his early attention.'[7] The problem was that his focus and determination were fundamentally misguided: 'He soon made it clear to officials that top of his list was one aspect of education that had figured prominently in Labour's election manifesto – secondary school reorganisation.'[8] As

Crosland put it in his seminal 1956 book *The Future of Socialism*: the tripartite system separated 'the unselected goats and the carefully selected sheep on the basis of tests which measure home backgrounds as much as innate ability'.[9]

For all that the proponents of comprehensive education had been gathering converts, by the time Crosland arrived at the DES in January 1965, very few of the 6000 state secondary schools had been converted or were even scheduled to convert. And the House of Commons resolution cited above was intended by the Prime Minister, Harold Wilson, simply as an expression of hot air to shut up the more driven Labour backbenchers – indeed, in 1963 Wilson had said: 'The grammar school will be abolished over my dead body.'[10] In 1957, a Labour Party opinion poll had found that a majority of the population was happy to continue with selective education and only 10 per cent thought it undesirable. As George Tomlinson, Labour's Minister of Education in 1947, said: 'the Party are kidding themselves if they think that the comprehensive idea has any popular appeal'. Looking back in 1971, Dennis Marsden wrote in the Fabian pamphlet *Politicians, Equality and Comprehensives*: 'Claims of a mandate for comprehensives were so much eyewash.' Indeed, the old and successful notion of the grammar school that emanated from the same liberal or Whig intellectual well as the Northcote–Trevelyan civil service reforms in the nineteenth century was enthusiastically adopted by Fabian socialists such as Sidney Webb and, later, R.H. Tawney, who saw grammar schools (because they were forced to select on the basis of ability rather than class) as the apotheosis of a socialist meritocracy, opening up opportunities to all on the basis of ability rather than parental wealth.

Crosland's appointment, however, changed everything. His predecessor, Michael Stewart, had gone through the motions of drafting a circular but with limited enthusiasm and even more limited effort. The real work started when Crosland took over, with discussion – or, to be more accurate, argument – centring on whether to 'require' or 'request' LEAs to reorganize their schools. For all Crosland's determination on the issue, he himself had argued in *The Future of Socialism* that the immediate abolition of grammar schools would produce too great a backlash and that only a voluntarily brought-about system would last.[11] As he put it in a speech in January 1966, Britain's education system was 'educationally and socially unjust, inefficient, wasteful and divisive . . . True equality of opportunity cannot be accomplished in one generation, or by education alone; it needs a wider social revolution.'[12]

But the circular gave LEAs a year to draw up their response, which meant, in some cases, a year of resistance. *The Times*, for instance, attacked the 'unrealizable ideal of equality'.[13] Some LEAs, such as Bournemouth, made it clear that they were having none of it. So the argument within the DES was over how to respond to this. In March 1966 Crosland issued a further circular stating that no building projects would be approved unless they fitted in with a comprehensive system. With the baby boom necessitating large building projects for schools to cope with the demand for places, this was not so much bribery as downright blackmail, given that Circular 10/65 was a supposedly voluntary request. So it was not surprising that by the deadline there were less than twenty LEAs which had not submitted the 'requested' plans. Counties such as Bromley and Surrey, which would ordinarily have had no truck with comprehensive schooling, caved in to financial necessity. As the *Times Educational Supplement* concluded when Crosland left the DES in September 1967: 'A great shove towards comprehensive schools has been given.'[14]

Not that one should misread the situation. When the political establishment – let alone the educational establishment – is solidly agreed on a received wisdom then it is almost always wrong. And make no mistake: even without the financial penalties, there was an overwhelming chattering-class consensus behind comprehensive schooling, although much of the support was based on ignorance, with some people thinking that somehow comprehensives would exist alongside grammar schools. And Butskellism – the de facto fusing of Labour and Conservative policy which characterized the 1950s – was, by the 1960s, fully at work in education. In 1963, the then Conservative Education Secretary, Edward Boyle, said that 'none of us believes in pre-war terms that children can be sharply differentiated into various types or levels of ability'.[15] Margaret Thatcher, appointed to the DES after the Conservative victory in June 1970, withdrew Circular 10/65 and replaced it with Circular 10/70, allowing each authority to decide its own attitude; but even she nonetheless closed more grammar schools (3286) than any other education minister. The Conservatives' 1970 manifesto expressed the party's pride that 'many of the most imaginative new schemes abolishing the 11-plus have been introduced by Conservative councils'.

The few grammar schools which still exist today had councils which placed the value of education higher than political and ideological dogma.

Some people associate a defence of grammar schools with looking back to a supposed 'golden age' of education. The truth is that there has never been such a period. Under the old tripartite system, secondary modern and technical schools were the poor relations of the grammar school and the system had major flaws. But there should be no doubt that grammar schools did the job they were supposed to do. For the first two thirds of the twentieth century, education was the great engine of social mobility. As state education improved, so did the chance of escaping from an upbringing of poverty. But the final third of the twentieth century saw a catastrophic decline in standards, causing a similar reduction in social mobility. Today, once more, where one is born on the social scale is by far the greatest determinant of where one will end up. Far from drawing the nation together, the educational revolution of the 1960s – essentially the introduction of comprehensive schools coupled with the forced implementation of 'progressive' teaching methods – led inexorably to an ever-growing educational apartheid.

The act of educational vandalism which destroyed all but the 164 grammar schools which survive today is the single worst political decision of the past 50 years, with terrible consequences from which we suffer every day, typified by the fact that one in five pupils now leaves school functionally illiterate and by the growing need for schools to employ their own police officer to deal with crimes committed on their premises. Instead of devising policies which would tackle the failures of secondary modern and technical schools, the political elites tore down the one glowingly successful class of school which had, for many of them, been their own ladder of opportunity.

The impact of this was made worse by the concurrent debasement of the exam system. Just as in Soviet Russia tractor production figures were always on the rise, so today we have an annual celebration of increasing exam passes and improving grades, all of which is built on a lie. As the Office of National Statistics reported in 2007, pupils capable of getting only a C in exams two decades ago can now expect an A grade. On average, A-levels for pupils of the same ability improved by two grades between 1988 and 2006. In maths – one of the core subjects – scores increased by more than three grades. In 2006, 24.1 per cent of all tests taken received the top grade; in the mid-80s just 9 per cent achieved A grades. At GCSE level, the report found that there was an increase of about a third of a grade between 1996 and 1998 for pupils of the same ability. At A-level a candidate given an F in maths in 1998 would, on average, get a C in 2005. Students of average ability in 1988 gained E grades in geography and biology and Ds in English literature, history and French. In 2005 teenagers of similar ability were awarded C grades in all subjects.[16] Maybe we are indeed getting cleverer as a species or being better taught; or maybe the grades are a fiction. The best universities certainly think the latter. As *The Times* reported in January 2008:

Top universities are drawing up blacklists of 'soft' A-level subjects that will bar applicants from winning places on their degree courses. They are warning that candidates who take more than one of the subjects such as accountancy, leisure studies and dance are unlikely to gain admission. They say they lack the academic rigour to prepare students for courses and are alarmed at the way increasing numbers of state schools are using them to boost pupils' top grades . . . Some universities such as the London School of Economics (LSE) and Cambridge University have already published lists of up to 25 subjects on their websites. Others are less overt but still operate lists. Wendy Piatt, director-general of the Russell Group of 20 leading universities, said most top institutions would follow suit in 'providing a steer on preferred combinations of A-levels'. She warned that a new analysis carried out by the group showed that a gulf was emerging between state and private schools, as comprehensives opted for 'soft' A-levels and independents and grammars tightened their grip on traditional academic subjects.[17]

None of this was inevitable. It was the result of a poisonous mix of educational dogma and political ideology. Other countries have managed without such problems. The reason? They were not afflicted by the disease which took over the British education establishment after the Second World War, which viewed education not as the passing on of knowledge and the skills required to think but as a key battleground in the process of transforming society. This led to a blueprint being drawn up which would, it was expected, impose the mechanism of that social engineering – comprehensive education to achieve equality – across the country.

The modern concept of compulsory, state-financed education arose in eighteenth-century Prussia, with the goal not of education and broadening the mind but of turning children into so-called 'human dough', to be placed on a 'social kneading board'. Although the language used by the twentieth-century social engineers was very different, the mindset was the same. The attitude was typified by Michael Young's famous *The Rise of the Meritocracy*, which argued that a country in which meritocracy was the determinant of social mobility would be profoundly unequal because it would simply lead to a new elite, leaving others to fester behind; thus, equality of opportunity should be replaced with equality of outcome – a line that Crosland swallowed hook, line and sinker. Comprehensive schooling would be the first line in that battle and would force children to be equal.

This went hand in hand with the sociological analysis which gripped the educational establishment during the first half of the twentieth century, which held that everything boiled down to class: educational failure was determined by schools' class bias. Ridiculous as it may seem now, there was a widespread view that if working-class children failed grammar or maths tests, they were simply resisting middle-class control. As one perceptive historian of the subject says: 'For both intellectual and practical reasons many educators were convinced that the solution to apparently intractable educational problems lay not in perseverance and meritocratic classification but in the abandonment of the syllabus and the celebration of working-class culture. And sometimes even of counter-cultural rebellion.'[18]

As Melanie Phillips points out in *All Must Have Prizes*, the impact of the First World War had been profound. Just about everything in society was thrown open to question. Anything which resembled Prussian attitudes was viewed as dangerously militaristic – and elements of education, with orderly rows of desks and multiplication tables, were thus viewed as suspect. Books such as *What Is And What Might Be* by Edmond Holmes, published in 1911, which argued that education was simply about fostering growth rather than imparting information, moved from being seen as wacky notions unfit for serious consideration to forward-thinking analyses of the mistakes of society. Holmes put it thus: 'The process of growing must be done by the growing organism, the child, let us say, and by no-one else . . . The forces that make for the child's growth come from within himself; and it is for him and him alone, to feed them, use them, evolve them.'[19] God forbid that the teacher should have such a role. By 1938, the Spens Report on Secondary Education was able to cite with approval an earlier report's demand that the curriculum 'should be thought of in terms of activity and experience rather than of knowledge to be acquired and facts to be stored'.[20] The sentiments in that one sentence embody the ruin of education which has followed.

The watershed for these developments was the Second World War, after which ideas which had merely been gaining piecemeal adherents became the norm. Why did it all come together then? Melanie Phillips explains:

The war had created a new sense of social solidarity. There was the desire to create a new society, a new social order based on fairness and social justice, accompanied by a deep sense of guilt among the middle classes that social class had deprived working-class children of their chance of success. There was the increasingly widespread impact of psychological theories of child-rearing which inspired deep guilt among adults about the harm done to children by repressing their personalities. There was the increasing influence of teacher-training colleges as teaching struggled to give itself higher professional status. There was the panic among teachers at having to control classrooms of children who didn't want to be at school at all but were captive pupils courtesy of the raising of the school-leaving age, a panic that made the teachers receptive to any suggested techniques that claimed to hold children's attention.[21]

The culmination of this was the Plowden Report into primary education, published in 1967. The report has come to be regarded as the foundation of progressive education; in truth, it simply drew together ideas which had already seized control of teacher-training colleges. Plowden put it thus: 'The school sets out . . . to devise the right environment for children, to allow them to be themselves and to develop in the way and at the pace appropriate to them. It tries to equalise opportunities and compensate for handicaps. It lays special stress on individual discovery, on first-hand experience and on opportunities for creative work. It insists that knowledge does not fall into neatly separate compartments and that work and play are not opposite but complementary.'[22] All that mattered was freeing the innate creative imagination of the child. As for imparting facts: other people's experiences were a waste of time. Only if a child had experienced something for itself or learned to empathize could it be said to understand something or be educated. Worse still, imposing facts – other people's experiences and assertions – was a deliberately destructive act, since it fettered a child's creativity. Take the writings of Caroline Gipps, now Vice Chancellor of the University of Wolverhampton but previously one of the most renowned educationalists in the land. In 1993 she informed us that learning 'is a process of knowledge construction, not of recording or absorption'.[23] So no multiplication table tests for her pupils, then?

This guff – today's received wisdom in educational theory – is absorbed at teacher-training colleges and then regurgitated in the classroom, condemning generations of pupils to ignorance of basic knowledge and to failure in life. No child must ever be told he or she is wrong. Every experience is by definition correct, because it is the child's own experience which matters. Literacy – being able to read and write in what was traditionally regarded as the proper manner – is merely an imposition on a child's creativity. As Peter Traves, an English adviser with Shropshire County Council, put it in a paper in 1991, such a definition of literacy was actually damaging. 'Proper literacy' involved bringing 'your knowledge and your experience to bear on what passes before you'. 'Improper literacy' was simply letting your eye look at the words on the page and your brain translate the symbols. 'Mere reading . . . is a reductive and destructive state of being in which the illusion of achievement is substituted for the genuine article, where the potential for power has been thwarted and channelled.'[24]

But, as Melanie Phillips shows, what turns this into something truly memorable is Mr Traves's remarks about his son, Richard: 'Richard's pre-school and nursery experience of reading was a very positive and fairly rich one. Although he went to school unable to "read" in the sense of being able to decode the print of books, he behaved as a reader in almost every other respect . . . He enjoyed being read to, talked about the stories and wanted more books. He memorised stories and large chunks of the phrasing from books and then delivered them back enthusiastically in a readerly tone of voice.'[25] It is difficult to know whether to laugh at the sheer idiocy of this man's supposedly serious views or to cry for poor Richard for being brought up by such a father. It gets worse when he describes Richard's school experience: 'Richard started at the bottom of the scheme and stayed there . . . He had seen himself as a reader. He now described himself not only as a non-reader but as generally stupid.' Poor Richard had no chance. Readers in Staffordshire will no doubt be delighted to learn that Mr Traves is now Corporate Director of Children and Lifelong Learning for Staffordshire County Council.

Wrapped up in this issue is the so-called debate between advocates of phonics and 'Look and Say' – in reality no more of a debate than that between those who argue that $2 + 2 = 4$ and those who say that $2 + 2 = 5$. Phonics is the label given to learning how to read through recognizing and sounding every letter and then reading them together to form words. 'Look and Say', on the other hand, requires children to recognize entire words from their context. The difference is that phonics works and 'Look and Say' doesn't, a fact which at last appears to have dawned on enough people to force the hands of educationalists who had rejected phonics. A seven-year study of schools in Clackmannanshire demonstrated conclusively – as if there were any doubt – that pupils taught to read through phonics were, by the age of eleven, on average three and a half years ahead for their age in reading and one year and eight months ahead in spelling. Boys outscored girls and there was almost no difference between pupils from different backgrounds. As one of the proponents of phonics, Ruth Miskin, showed when teaching in East London, even in a school where almost every pupil was Bangladeshi, and for whom English was a second language, by the age of six every one of them could read fluently.

But even with the supposed improvements to 'bog-standard comprehensives' under Labour, such as the introduction in 1998 of the National Literacy Strategy, almost 1.2 million children have failed to achieve the expected levels of literacy. In 2005, only 56 per cent of 11-year-old boys and 71 per cent of girls in England managed to reach the standard expected for their age. When will we learn that one method works and that not teaching that method is, in condemning so many children to illiteracy, a form of child abuse?

Not that it was just literacy which was infected with the virus of progressive teaching. Maths has suffered even more. The same notions of creativity and relevance have been applied to mathematics and have led to a similar collapse in standards. Scores of less than 20 per cent on a GCSE paper are now enough to gain a C pass, even under an already reduced standard of examination. The think-tank Reform analysed O-level/GCSE examinations from 1951. It found that until 1970 they were 'a rigorous test of thought and initiative in algebra, arithmetic and geometry. Students were required to think for themselves.' By 1980, questions were starting to become simpler.

> Following the introduction of the GCSE there was a sharp drop in difficulty, with questions leading pupils step by step to a solution. Pass marks were lowered throughout the period ... Relevance has replaced rigour in the belief that this would make mathematics more accessible. At the same time high stakes assessment has reduced what should be a coherent discipline to 'pick 'n' mix', with pupils being trained to answer specific shallow questions on a range of topics where marks can be most easily harvested.[26]

And when teachers are recruited to teach knowledge in schools which place a value on high standards, their influence can be worse than useless, since many teachers themselves suffer the consequences of their own education. Dr Martin Stephen, High Master of St Paul's School, relates that: 'Subject knowledge has become the poor relation of teaching, a once elemental requirement that for several years has been kicked into touch.' He describes what happened at recent job interviews.

> At my school, we make all teaching job applicants teach a specimen lesson. They are given details a week in advance, and the topic is deliberately simple and straightforward. Twice recently, we have been thrilled to interview candidates for science teaching posts with a 2:1 in their subject from a highly regarded university, and five

or six years' experience. The lessons were catastrophic, riddled with basic factual errors. The head of department, observing the lessons, confiscated the pupils' notes, for fear they might regurgitate them at GCSE.[27]

As a guide for trainee teachers published by the London Institute of Education – home of many of the country's most influential educationalists – asserted, schools are guilty of too often 'legitimising one popular view of mathematics' – arithmetic, algebra and geometry – and so devaluing 'the students' informal mathematical experience and skills . . . which are equally, if not more, valuable to the individual'. Maths is oppressive; it should be replaced by 'ethnomathematics', since 'the view that "official" mathematics dominates "ethnomathematics" is consistent with that of Western cultural/educational imperialism in mathematics education'.[28] Our everyday experiences are what maths is really about, not the pedagogic instructions of a teacher. As the headmaster in Lambeth who appointed an expert in Nigerian cooking, with no experience of maths teaching, to teach maths in his school expressed it: 'It is real life maths with Ibo cookery – transferable maths.'[29] The consequence is that:

The UK, home of Turing, father of modern information technology and numerous recent prize winners such as Atiyah and Wiles, is failing to generate sufficient quality mathematicians. Financial services are being forced to recruit a high proportion of overseas graduates – as many as seven out of eight of all such posts. UK workplaces are finding themselves short of people with basic mathematics skills. Universities are being asked to select from a significantly reduced pool of applicants, a large number of whom are independently educated or from overseas.[30]

'The progressive classroom,' writes Adrian Wooldridge, 'was a laboratory of the classless society – an idyllic place in which co-operation flourished and competition was unknown. Nothing angers progressive teachers quite so much as testing, which, they argue, measures little more than social background and so simply perpetuates and justifies social inequalities. Children who are labelled as failures at primary school are likely to go on to fulfil their own low expectations. The yobs on the football terraces were venting their anger at those nasty spelling tests.'[31] The state school classroom has in many instances become an unfamiliar environment to those who work on the basis of fact and reason.

These horror stories demonstrate the damage done by the divorce of the professional classes from the state system. The disease was able to take hold because there was no professional class involved to protest. When the French state system was threatened by such ideas, all parties were motivated to mobilize to prevent any damage because each had a stake in the system. And it was a left-wing politician, the socialist Jean-Pierre Chevènement (dubbed France's Tony Benn), who as Minister of Education in France led the fight against these 'progressive' notions through his policy of *élitisme républicain* (elitism for all). For the 'paradox of Plowdenism', as Wooldridge calls it, is that it strengthens the class divisions it is supposed to tear down. Poor children are less equipped to deal with the unstructured, loose environment of such schools than their middle-class peers, whose confidence typically sees them through alien experiences and whose parents often compensate for the failure of teachers and schools to do their job.

One key reason why these theories have continued to wreak havoc for so long is that the Department for Education (or whatever it is called under its latest rebranding) has been a bastion of these ideas and has fought in the trenches to resist the march of common sense. From the Whitehall centre down to Local Education Authorities, ideological enforcers have ensured that challengers to the worship of comprehensives and adherence to progressive dogmas were silenced. Melanie Phillips' *All Must Have Prizes* details a notorious example of this in 1987, when the history department at Lewes Priory school sought to switch from the vacuous GCSE to the more rigorous Scottish O-grade. The school authorities went berserk, barring the teachers even from discussing the idea with parents outside of school hours and effectively sacking them. They were then blacklisted from further employment in the state sector. Similarly, any educationalist who does not support the prevailing tenets of progressive education is smeared and attacked by supposedly neutral civil servants. Sir Geoffrey Holland, Permanent Secretary from 1993 to 1994, made clear after his retirement that the department was entirely in thrall to the received wisdom: schools' priority should be 'learning, not teaching . . . The world these young people are going to own and live in is not a world in which people sit neatly and tidily in separate rooms in rows, and change every forty minutes from one subject to another . . .

It is a world . . . where the teacher has to become the supporter of the learner which requires a fundamental reversal of the traditional role of the teacher.'[32] Another senior civil servant in the department is quoted by Melanie Phillips as referring to the 'fundamental and philosophical divide' in education and the 'battle' against non-believers in which his department is engaged.[33] And to make things worse, campaigners against the rot adopted completely the wrong approach, campaigning in the 1980s for a national curriculum through which sense would, in theory, be legislated into schools. Instead, all that happened was that the levers of centralized control were made far, far stronger than ever before and ensured that the infection was even more widespread in its impact.

There were, of course, those who argued that comprehensive schools and progressive teaching methods were a good thing on their own educational merits; that the way to overcome the failure of the secondary modern schools was to destroy the grammar schools, force high achievers into mixed-ability classes and schools and watch the less academic pupils improve. But we are still waiting for that to happen. What has happened instead is that high achievers have not been stretched as they were in grammar schools, some potential high achievers have been lost in the morass, and low achievers have been condemned to remain at the bottom of the pile. There has been no specific statistical survey in the UK to analyse the respective merits of selective and mixed-ability teaching. However, the most extensive related survey, carried out by Professor John Marks in 1991, demonstrated that: 'Public examination statistics for Northern Ireland [where selection continued] show a very different pattern from those for England and Wales. Starting from a much lower base, the proportion of leavers with A-level and good O-level results rose steeply during the 1950s and 1960s and continued to rise rapidly until well into the 1970s. There was no plateau after 1970 as found in England and Wales and the figures for Northern Ireland are now anything from 30 per cent to 50 per cent higher than those for England and Wales.'[34]

The comprehensive monolith, even with the variations and revisions adopted by the Labour government under Tony Blair, has nothing to offer the parent caught in the now classic trap of being concerned about their child's schooling but unable either to pay for private education or to move to a better catchment area for a half-decent school. Grammar schools, on the other hand, put on a formal footing as open to all who were bright enough to attend by the Butler Education Act of 1944, enabled working-class children to mix with their similarly able middle-class peers.

What a terrible irony; the 1944 Act, which enshrined the idea of a grammar-school place for the intellectually able rather than the socially well connected, was the culmination of the arguments of socialists such as Sidney Webb and R.H. Tawney. Instead of wrecking the achievements of grammar schools and levelling everyone down, the response to the failures of the system should have been to extend their ethos and emphasis on qualifications and standards to the second-ary modern sector, emulating the achievement of Germany and Holland in particular, with their vocational schools. Comprehensive schools have simply replaced selection by ability with selection by class and house price. Middle-class children now go to middle-class comprehensives, whose catchment areas comprise middle-class neighbourhoods, and working-class children are left to fester in the inner city comprehensive their parents cannot afford to move away from.

'Can we not learn,' wrote the philosopher John Gray, 'from the Asian tigers that economic success in our time demands an education system that rewards ability, rather than one in which egalitarianism and privilege co-exist and reinforce one another? Can we not see how egalitarian policies in state schools help to reproduce elites for which the Britain in which the majority of us live might as well be a foreign land?'[35] The answer to both of Professor Gray's questions is a resounding 'no'.

4

FOOD

8 October 1945

On 8 October 1945, a small American defence contractor, Raytheon, filed a US patent. It was not for one of its usual categories of weapons. It was for a method of cooking.

Two British scientists – Professors Randall and Boot of Birmingham University – had invented the cavity magnetron, which enabled a process by which short-wave – 'microwave' – radar could detect enemy aircraft. What the British could not crack, however, was how to mass-produce the magnetron tube which formed the basis of the radar's operation. This was a critical need: the radar enabled the user to 'see' at night, while the Nazis – without the radar – were effectively flying blind. Having the radar would give the RAF an enormous advantage in repelling the Luftwaffe night raids, but this would require tens of thousands of the tubes.

Raytheon had already begun experimenting with microwave tubes and one of the company's scientists, Percy Spencer, had been building a new tube – a magnetron – for a radar machine. Spencer was the world's leading expert in magnetron tubes and a meeting was set up between the scientist and his British counterparts. Spencer was self-taught but he succeeded where the Brits and all the main US corporations had failed. In the course of one weekend he created a production process that both improved the functioning of the tube and was speedy enough to facilitate mass production. Thanks to Spencer, by 1945 Raytheon was producing 80 per cent of all magnetrons, leaving Western Electric, RCA, GE and all the other giants of US electrical manufacturing far behind.

But there was more to Spencer's work than merely inventing a process that helped save the free world. As he was working on the tube, a chocolate peanut bar in Spencer's pocket started to melt. He realized immediately what had happened: the microwaves had heated it. Intrigued, he started to experiment and put some popcorn near the tube. It popped. The next day, he tried putting an egg near the tube. A colleague joined him to watch. The egg soon started to shake. The colleague peered towards it to get a closer look. At that moment, it exploded and deposited hot yolk on his face. Spencer realized he had happened upon something interesting. He then cut an opening in a metal box, through which he fed microwaves, creating a high-density electromagnetic field. As he filled the box with microwaves, the food heated very quickly.

Using the technology invented by Spencer, Raytheon built a test oven, to be tried out in a Boston restaurant. The test went well and by 1947 the company had built the first commercial microwave oven, the Radarange. (The name was thought up by an employee in a competition.) The fundamental process may have been the same as in today's domestic microwave ovens but that was about all they had in common: the Radarange was 6 feet tall, weighed 750 pounds, used 3000 watts (three times as much as today's), was water-cooled (and so had to be plumbed in) and cost $5000. The first realistic commercial microwave oven went on sale in 1954, without the need for water-cooling and using half the wattage, selling for $2000. The following year, the Tappan Stove Company began selling, under licence, the first domestic microwave oven. But the $1300 price was still prohibitive and sales were poor. Four years later, in 1958, the first commercial microwave oven went on sale in the UK, produced by C.E. Tibbs, the founder of Merrychef, which today is the largest producer of microwaves in the EU.

It was, however, only in the late 1960s that the technology really took off, with the counter-top 100-volt Radarange selling for $495. It was not only smaller and cheaper than previous models, but was also safer and more reliable. Restaurants and vending companies could immediately see the benefits. They could keep products in the fridge and then heat to order. Since typical cooking times were one fifth of those for conventional cooking methods, the advantage was obvious, and even more so if food was kept in the freezer rather than the fridge: instead of having to throw away any unused refrigerated food, frozen food could simply be kept for another day. Housewives grabbed the chance to shorten the time spent cooking, one of the most time-consuming household tasks, and the new, cheaper model led to a domestic-market explosion. New food products also emerged to take advantage of this new form of cooking. Crisps, coffee beans and peanuts were all dried using microwaves. And meat could be defrosted before being sold; it could even be pre-cooked and sold for the housewife to reheat.

Technological advances and redesigns (to the now omnipresent short, wide shape) sparked a further acceleration in the market. In 1970, 40,000 were sold in the US; by 1975 a million had been bought. In Japan, sales were even greater. The first of these domestic microwaves went on sale in the UK in 1974. The new technology made them cheaper to produce and the relative cheapness of microprocessors meant electronic controls could be added for little extra cost. Today, almost every home has a microwave. To which you might ask: so what? Why is the ubiquity of a cooking process so important?

This news report, from the *Observer* in December 2007, helps explain it:

A multimillion-pound campaign to encourage Britons to eat five portions of fruit and vegetables a day has flopped, a government report will reveal this week. Most people are still ignoring official advice to change their diets in a bid to help ward off cancer, heart disease and other illnesses, an inquiry by the Prime Minister's Strategy Unit has discovered. The unit says that reluctance to eat enough fruit and vegetables is causing 42,200 premature deaths a year and costing the NHS £6 billion annually to treat diseases linked to poor diet . . .

The report, the first Gordon Brown commissioned from the Strategy Unit after becoming Prime Minister in the summer, says poor diet kills 69,400 Britons every year – 10 per cent of all deaths. As well as the 42,200 linked to a lack of fruit and vegetables, 20,200 are due to excess salt consumption, while 3,500 are linked to an intake of saturated fats and 3,500 to excessive sugar consumption.[1]

Or this: 'The Office for National Statistics changes its 650-strong basket of goods and services [most widely bought] once a year to include more up-to-date items . . . [In 2006] the 'out' list includes the dining room table – because families no longer eat meals together.'[2]

Or these random figures:

Ninety-one per cent of all British homes have a microwave oven.[3]

A quarter of UK households no longer own a dining table; a third of Britons say they do not eat vegetables because they take too much effort to prepare; Britons eat more ready meals than the rest of the EU put together; 40 per cent of patients entering hospital are diagnosed as suffering from malnutrition; only 40 per cent of parents regularly eat with their children; 50 per cent of meals eaten in Britain are eaten alone; Britain eats more than half of all the savoury snacks eaten in Europe.[4]

None of the statistics are, of course, random. They are all interrelated. They stem from one disastrous and, within Europe, almost uniquely British phenomenon: the collapse of cooking skills. And that stems in large measure from the – again, almost uniquely British – spread of the microwave and the replacement of traditional cooking with ready meals heated in the microwave.

So deep-seated is this now that in 2005 Dame Deidre Hutton, then chair of the Food Standards Agency, argued – rightly – that this was having a detrimental impact on health. But such is the mindset today that she went on to argue not that this implied the necessity of real cooking with real ingredients, but that ready meals should be more nutritious: 'Processed food is here to stay . . . [I]t is no good trying to take people back to some largely mythical golden age.'[5] Mythical? It certainly wasn't a golden age and traditional British food might have been pilloried, but dishes such as toad-in-the-hole, roast beef and Yorkshire pudding, hotpot, shepherd's pie, stew, cauliflower cheese, bangers and mash, steak and kidney pudding and other traditional British dishes were cooked by real people in real kitchens using real ingredients, eaten on real dining tables and provided real and regular nutritious meals. Today, such is the collapse in cookery skills that, as Joanna Blythman reports: 'One senior manager in a large north-eastern company building homes for the middle to upper end of the housing market told me how they operated a "buy back" scheme in which someone who buys a new-build house can trade it in for another new-build house a few years later. "When we get the houses back we are surprised by how many people have never used the oven. We know this because the instruction manuals are still inside."'[6]

TV chefs are now so successful and popular that they are identified by their Christian names alone – Jamie, Delia and

Gordon – but although they may have widened the culinary horizons of some parts of the middle classes, their success is largely built on a culture in which their viewers are happy to sit in front of their TVs munching their way through plates of what is often little better than swill. As one of the country's leading chefs and food writers, Simon Hopkinson, puts it: 'Something seems to be ever so slightly rotten in the state of the British kitchen just now. I sometimes feel that we have all but lost the grasp of how to cook nicely at all. We watch endless cookery programmes but prefer, finally, to spend lots of money on supermarket ready-meals while idly turning the pages of spotlessly clean cookery books until the microwave pings.'[7]

Indeed, even chefs no longer always cook. Rare is the restaurant that does not get a daily delivery from the likes of companies such as 3663 and Brakes, delivering cook-chilled prepared dishes which the 'chef' need only heat up on serving. As 3663's website explains:

> 3663 First for Foodservice is the UK's leading food-service company with sales of over £1 billion a year. We deliver quality ingredients, finished products and equipment to the catering industry. In all, over 6,800 people manage 1.84 million square feet of storage in 40 depots across the country. A modern fleet of 1,100 vehicles deliver to over 50,000 customers. No one offers local customers the same breadth of services as 3663. We provide dedicated frozen, fresh and chilled and full multi-temperature delivery with the flexibility, speed of response and local knowledge that are vital to our customers.[8]

Quite. If your chef can't poach an egg or make mayonnaise, no need to worry. He doesn't have to. All that is required of him is to heat up the delivery made in the morning. And if making a burger is way too advanced, no matter.

This is of a piece with the attitude that food is something that arrives in a packet and is heated up, rather than a selection of ingredients that are cooked. It is not widely considered necessary to teach children how to cook. At home, it is not simply thought unnecessary; it is often an impossibility, when there is no one capable of teaching them. And at school, it is no longer even thought desirable. It used to be that Home Economics was a regular part of the curriculum. But this was considered infra dig: the national curriculum was not concerned with such fripperies as learning how to boil an egg or make an apple pie. And so, in the 1990s, Home Economics was replaced with Food Technology, in which pupils learned to 'interact successfully with materials, tools and resources'.

Joanna Blythman's investigation of the decline of British food, *Bad Food Britain*, cites this revealing explanation of what Food Technology is really about from Ali Farrell of the 'Food Forum': 'The domestic context is no longer the only relevant one. A great deal happens to food before it reaches our homes which impacts on its quality, and there are more food options available to us than in the past . . . It is just as important for today's young people to be conversant with the issues surrounding food as it is to be able to boil an egg.'[9] This is, of course, the same drivel as the ideology which has infected core curriculum subjects such as history, where learning what happened, when and why is considered less relevant to today's needs than empathizing with the experience of a blind, one-legged peasant during the 100 Years' War.

Food Technology, however, does not actually involve contact with food. As Joanna Blythman has shown, *Collins Total Revision Guide for GCSE Food and Technology* explains what the subject actually covers. Pupils must 'design and make' a new product for sale, using 'Information Communication Technology', 'Computer Aided Design', 'Computer Aided Manufacture' and 'Computer Integrated Manufacture' in moving from an idea to sale. Forget about baking a cake. Instead, they conceive a new cake-based product and plot its course through manufacture to sale, even though they may never in their lives have seen, let alone used, flour.

What messages do children take from this? That food is made in factories by quasi-scientists as part of a commercial process. And that what matters is not smell and taste but the right use-by date. It is no wonder that a government survey in 2003 found that people in their early twenties were unlikely to shop at grocers', butchers' and markets because: 'They express anxiety about entering environments that do not have pre-packed produce available.'[10] And it should come as no surprise that a National Farmers' Union survey in 1999 found that nearly half of all children thought margarine came from a cow and nearly a quarter had no idea that bread contained flour. Similarly, a British Heart Foundation report in 2005 found that 36 per cent of children had no idea that chips were made from potatoes (indeed, the British Potato Council discovered that 60 per cent of children thought potatoes grew on trees).[11]

It is a vicious circle. Demand for microwave-cooked meals rose by 70 per cent between 1994 and 2004[12] and by

2003 Britons ate 49 per cent of the combined total of all such meals eaten in Europe.[13] But the more we eat of these meals, the more we end up with little alternative to them, as even the basic skills required to cook disappear. And when the ready meals we see before us have the allure of the premium range, why would we care? In 2005 the *Guardian* found that Sainsbury's 'Taste the Difference' Luxury Shepherd's Pie, 'based on the famous Ivy restaurant's recipe' – Yummy! Not just a bog-standard shepherd's pie but one eaten by posh people – was maybe not quite so luxurious after all, since it contained sixty-nine ingredients such as chemical flavouring, preservatives, hardened fats and dextrin.[14] Next time you hear Dervla Kirwan's preposterously sultry Irish brogue sensually eulogizing not just any food but Marks and Spencer's food, remember that while the food she is urging you to buy may be free of artificial colouring or flavours, what you are looking at has as much in common with home-cooked food as Millwall does with Real Madrid.

It is sometimes impossible to believe how quickly things have changed. British food may long have been sneered at the world over but the legacy of the war and rationing made, at the very least, the British housewife an expert at utilizing ingredients. And by the time rationing ended in the 1950s, the role of the housewife was seen as something almost glamorous and exciting. Magazines and adverts portrayed her as attractive and satisfied in her position. As the historian Nicola Humble describes it:

> Hers was a marvellous new home, one of the 300,000 built every year throughout the 1950s, with many

labour-saving features (simple clean lines, with no picture rails or elaborate mouldings to catch dust, and appliances galore). Particularly splendid was its kitchen, for the kitchen was at the centre of the 1950s domestic dream, the place where the young wife bound her husband to her with her culinary skills, where she supported his business career by producing impressive dinners for his boss and clients, where the mother prepared for the family bonding ritual that was the daily evening meal.[15]

Almost no aspect of this remains today – and certainly not the main component, the family meal, a fact confirmed by the ending in 1999 of that TV institution, the Oxo advert, which had featured a family sitting around a dining table eating a roast with Oxo gravy. In 1997 a poll found that two thirds of families ate in front of the TV.[16] Jonathan Meades explains this to readers of *The Times*: 'A "table" is an inanimate quadruped where people ate in the olden days. It has been replaced by street, couch, car (when not picking nose).'[17] This has implications that go far beyond the simple act of eating and impacts on all aspects of children's behaviour – and, thus, eventually on adult behaviour. The very bonds of family life are diminished when eating is merely a refuelling opportunity rather than a family occasion.

Indeed, not only do children not eat at the table with their family, but what they eat is also – a peculiarly British trait – very different from anything eaten by adults. In restaurants, while adults eat their (often pre-cooked) chicken or beef dish, children eat from a separate 'children's menu', usually consisting of chicken nuggets and junior burgers and chips. And when, heaven forbid, no such menu is available, the child wails and screams and its parents complain about the cheek of a restaurant that so wilfully fails to provide for children. Contrast the British child in a restaurant with the French, Italian or Spanish child, for whom the only difference in food is a smaller portion and who sits at the table and eats like a properly socialized human being rather than a screaming monster. But then the foreign child is used to eating at a table with adults, because in his or her country the concept of the family meal remains alive.

At school, as Jamie Oliver made all too clear in his *Jamie's School Dinners* exposé on TV, children are dished up what can barely be described as food and is, rather, fried, reconstituted chemical compounds. In 2003, the average spend on a primary-school meal was 35 pence – a quarter of the sum spent on feeding an army dog.[18] Not that parents pay that. Usually they give four or five times that sum to the school but, to the powers that be in most schools, lunch is seen not as an opportunity to provide nutritious food but instead as a source of income to be spent on other areas of school life. As for packed lunches: the typical lunch box is made up of a sandwich on cheap white bread, some chocolate and some crisps. Compare that with continental meals, where pupils are given normal, nutritious adult food – perhaps a salad, some cheese, some smoked fish with vegetables and a yoghurt or fruit.

Not, of course, that it is only British children who eat Turkey Twizzler food. One of the most depressing chains of shops is Best of British, a grocer in France that supplies expats with the supposed best of British. To look at their website is to despair.[19] 'Do you miss your favourite British food?' Don't worry – thanks to Best of British you don't have to miss out on the delights of Pilgrim Mild Cheddar, Atora Herby Dumpling Mix, Fray Bentos Steak and Kidney Pie, Pot Noodles and other such British delights. It is barely imaginable that any being with functional taste buds would choose to eat Pilgrim Mild Cheddar at all; but in France? Is it any wonder that we have taken so easily to microwave heated dishes when even Brits who live in France, a country with marvellous food easily available in local markets, still crave the rubbish they were used to at home?

The British have now developed a warped attitude to food. We will eat any old junk if it is nicely presented ready for the microwave or oven. Yet we live in constant fear of E. coli, pesticides, dioxins, BSE, CJD, GM foods or whatever else has been most recently depicted as the bad boy of nutrition, whether it be salt, sugar or dairy produce. Best, we think, to leave it to the supermarket to take care; after all, they wouldn't be allowed to sell it if it wasn't safe. And we gawp at freak shows such as Gillian McKeith's *You Are What You Eat*, in which grossly obese participants' poo is sent off for examination, as a result of which they are then told to eat alfalfa for the rest of their lives by a woman whose only relevant 'qualifications' are degrees from the Clayton College of Natural Health, an institution not recognized by the US Secretary for Education for the purpose of educational grants. Our attitude to food swings from one extreme to the other; the idea of a normal balanced diet never seems to cross anyone's mind. Not surprising, really, when an organization like the Food Standards Agency spends a fortune not educating but scaring children about food. Its bizarre website for children, Food Hygiene Mission Control, is almost as frightening as *Dr Who*.[20] Characters such as Safe-T are on a mission to exterminate Pathogens, the enemy. And on their mission they have to escape the clutches of 'risk', 'poisoning', 'contamination' and other enemies. Is it any wonder we have such a weird attitude to food when the government thinks its role is to brainwash children into being frightened of it?

And when as adults we are confronted with real food, we react like children: eeeuuuuggghhhh! When Gordon Ramsay demonstrated how to kill a live lobster on TV, Channel 4 was flooded with complaints. The nation went berserk when Jamie Oliver slaughtered a lamb, because food comes, we like to think, in pristine sealed containers. Fish is gutted and filleted. Chicken is neatly sliced into breasts. Blood is nowhere to be seen. Joanna Blythman writes of research carried out for the Institute of Grocery Distribution in 1998, which showed that supermarket shoppers want their meat 'presented in a sterile package format, with minimal reminders of the animal from which it was derived'.[21] And yet not long ago our grandparents not only ate brains, heart and liver; they relished them and prepared them themselves.

One further aspect of this childishness needs consideration: our attitude to alcohol. The likelihood is that for anyone under the age of about thirty, the definition of a good night out is one with the sole purpose of getting drunk. And what used to be a primarily male obsession – going down the boozer and getting hammered – is now an equal-opportunities activity: between 1988 and 2001, the number of women drinking more than 14 units a week rose by over 50 per cent. Alcohol abuse costs the NHS £1.7 billion a year, with 150,000 alcohol-related hospital admissions annually; between midnight and 5 a.m., alcohol is responsible for 70 per cent of all A&E admissions. Between 1996 and 2006, the number of children under 16 admitted with alcohol-related conditions increased by 29 per cent; and 60 per cent of those admitted were girls.[22] Because getting drunk is now seen as the definition of a good night, 18- to 25-year-olds are now regularly drinking five times the recommended daily limit.

The bald statistics, though, miss the point. We know we're drinking too much and we like it. As a nation, we go out specifically to get drunk. That's what it is today to be British. For the sheer foulness of the atmosphere, you'd have to go some to beat London's West End after about 11 p.m. The streets smell of piss. Boozed-up twenty-somethings roam the area, some throwing up, others looking as if they can barely stand. And all in the pervasive ambience of impending violence (it's no wonder that the British Crime Survey shows that only 16 per cent of violent acts by strangers are prompted by drugs, as opposed to 53 per cent by alcohol). The same picture holds true in other city centres and, increasingly, in rural villages. Unless you're drunk, Britain is a pretty disgusting place after the pubs shut.

Wander at night, however, in Europe's most beautiful squares, such as the Grande Place in Brussels, and you'll see a very different sight. In the summer, no matter how late it is, there will be tables outside and groups of friends sitting, talking and enjoying themselves over bottles of wine or Belgian beer. The rest of the year the same thing happens, just indoors. And without a hint of violence.

The explanation lies in the difference between a café culture and a pub culture. On the continent, alcohol may be an aid to the success of an evening, but the amount drunk is not the measure of that success. We, however, drink to get drunk and arrange affairs to do that as efficiently as possible. And children are taught from an early age to drink in their respective cultural tradition. As the chef Raymond Blanc (born in France but living in Britain) puts it: 'In all Latin countries, we drink with food; we hardly ever drink without food. That is an English invention.'[23]

The failure to educate children in how to eat is mirrored by the failure to inculcate in children and young adults a sensible attitude to alcohol. Because just as we race to get alcohol inside us, so too we have a rushed attitude to eating. In 1980, the average meal took an hour to prepare; today it takes an average of thirteen minutes and is predicted to take eight minutes by 2010.[24] Because we are not cooking meals: we are microwaving ready-prepared assemblages. We are supposedly all now in a rush. But this is nothing new: the situation was no different when convenience food first took off in the 1960s, prompting a glut of cookbooks for the cheap and quick meal. Take this from Erin Pizzey's *Slut's Cook Book*: 'Don't force your children to eat your carefully prepared home-made stews when what they really want is fish fingers and beans (which are just as nutritious anyway) . . . [G]et them a take-away when you can afford it.'[25]

By far the most successful example of this attitude was Delia Smith's 1971 breakthrough book *How to Cheat at Cooking*. (Her subsequent TV series was the now bafflingly titled *Family Fare*.) The sole aim of the book was to help the reader use convenience foods and 'at the same time convince everyone that they're strictly homemade ... There are more important things in life than cooking ... Never do for yourself what you can get someone else to do for you.'[26] Although Delia Smith's subsequent books were more concerned with home cooking than cheating, her first book's title sums up her baleful influence in a nutshell: the idea that proper cooking skills are a waste of time, to be avoided through short cuts. Ms Smith's influence on food in Britain has been almost entirely malign. Where the likes of Jamie Oliver and Nigel Slater enthuse about flavours and do their best to fight the onward march of microwave pap by encouraging people to enjoy food, to taste it and to cook with the results of that enjoyment and taste, Delia reinforces the idea that cooking is soulless, is a chore and is, in the end, pointless. Where Jamie Oliver and Nigel Slater paint with their food, Delia Smith cooks by numbers. The result is bland, lifeless and destructive to the idea that cooking is both a pleasure and a *good thing*.

Unthreatening her image may be, but the Delia attitude is a cousin to the feminist reaction to the image of the 1950s housewife discussed earlier. Take Pat Mainardi of the feminist group Redstockings: 'Women have been brainwashed more than even we can imagine. Men have no such conditioning. They recognize the essential fact of housework right from the very beginning. Which is that it stinks.'[27] But, as Joanna Blythman points out: 'No distinction was drawn between cooking a meal and clearing up a baby's vomit.'[28] And why, now, should cooking be thought of as the woman's preserve? Men are fully capable of turning a microwave on, and do – that is the whole point. We no longer eat together but as we see fit, in front of *Coronation Street* or the football.

Perhaps the most notable aspect of the first *How to Cheat* – the sainted Delia brought out a successor with the same title in 2008 – is its obsession with status and class. Take Delia's comments on the right drink to serve at a dinner party: 'Vermouth is a pretty safe bet. I'd be surprised if at least one guest didn't ask "What is it?" so choose an example that will give you a chance to drop the name of your wine-merchant (don't say off-licence).'[29] Class in Britain today remains notably alive when it comes to food. As regards the weekly shop, for instance, the supermarkets are decidedly class-based (although Tesco is now so vast that it stretches across the classes). Waitrose is at the top of the pile; Sainsbury's is a comfortable pair of slippers for its classless middle classes; Asda and Morrisons trade on their reputation for no-nonsense northern value; Netto, Aldi and Lidl take this to extremes. And the dishes they sell have their own class divide, with Tesco offering 'Value' goods for the hoi polloi and 'Finest' for those who want to think they are a cut above the rest and like to imagine they are eating especially well.

As for the tastes they cater to: a review by Tom Stoppard of Ernest Hemingway's posthumously published novel *The Garden of Eden* quoted Hemingway's mouthwatering description of a Spanish dish: 'It came in a large bowl with ice floating with the slices of crisp cucumber, tomato, garlic bread and red peppers, and the coarsely peppered liquid that tasted lightly of oil and vinegar. "It's salad soup," Catherine said. "It's delicious." "Es gazpacho," the waiter said.' Stoppard continued: 'Well, it isn't Hemingway's fault

that you can now get the stuff in cans at Safeway.'[30] And
there is another wonderful example of this in *From Russia
With Love* by Ian Fleming. James Bond is taken to an
incredibly exotic meal in the best restaurant in Turkey – 'a
little place in the Spice Bazaar'. Bond is led through 'a
maze of small, colourfully tiled, vaulted rooms to where
Kerim was sitting at a corner table over the entrance to the
bazaar'. Kerim, the master spy, translates the waiter's sug-
gestion: 'He says the Doner Kebab is very good today.'
With one bound, we jump from the mysterious East to a
greasy takeaway off the Goldhawk Road.[31]

Not that food is considered worth spending real money
on. In 2005, Wayne Rooney's then girlfriend was spotted
shopping in Kwik Save. As Martin Samuel commented in
The Times:

There was a photograph in the Sunday newspapers,
a standard pap snap, of Coleen McLoughlin, Wayne
Rooney's girlfriend, out shopping. No change there, you
might think. Over the past few years Coleen has enjoyed
a romance with retail that makes Michael Jackson look
frugal . . . So 'Coleen shops' is hardly big news. The
story was her choice of store. Kwik Save, Liverpool. No
clue to what she was buying, but it was unlikely to be the
work of hot designers V & R or the latest Franck Muller
timepiece. So a wild guess would suggest that Coleen
was on the lookout for cheap food, bringing her neatly
into line with the rest of modern Britain. A nation drib-
bling mass-produced ready meals down its designer tops.
A population of bleeding hearts that want animals to be
treated ethically but would rather eat a tin of condemned

veal than put 2p per pound on a packet of chicken drum-sticks. Have you seen the price of free-range meat? Get back in the cage the lot of you ... The future Mrs Rooney may only have stopped for some cheap booze and a Toilet Duck. But no footballer's wife would be seen dead leaving H. Samuel or British Home Stores. If Viktor & Rolf really want to crack the British market, maybe they should throw in a packet of fish fingers with the next collection.[32]

The British may never have had a continental élan in their food and may never have supported the range and quality of ingredients that remain available in continental markets, but there was, once, a range of artisanal producers and specialist retailers who provided high-quality local shopping. No town was without its fishmonger or butcher. They provided produce which was the staple of the British meal at table. All were skilled – even the local greengrocer – with their produce. Today, if you have a specific request, someone in the supermarket looks at the label to find what you are asking for. And that is as likely to be a snack as it is a meal. The average Brit eats 7.2 kg of snacks every year; an Italian eats just 1 kg.[33] We eat 6000 million bags of crisps and 4400 million other savoury snacks every year as well as spending £6.1 billion on sweets. So it should come as no surprise that the rate of obesity has quadrupled in the UK. In England, 22 per cent of men and 23 per cent of women were classified as clinically obese in 2002, while 43 per cent of men and 34 per cent of women were overweight. Among children, the rates of obesity have tripled during the last twenty years. One in ten children aged between four and five is obese and 13 per cent are overweight, with the figures rising to 17.5 per cent and 14.2 per cent by the age of eleven.[34] Seventeen per cent of fifteen-year-olds are obese. If present trends continue, it has been estimated that half of all children in England could be obese by 2020.[35]

The reason? Look no further than the rectangular box in the kitchen.

5

POLITICS

24 January 1981

Nearly every major development in British politics in the past three decades can be traced back to the events of one day: 24 January 1981, when the Labour Party held a special conference to draw up a new procedure for electing the party's leader and deputy leader.

The result of that conference marked the triumph of the 'loony left' in the party and led to Labour's 1983 manifesto, dubbed by the party's acerbic MP Gerald Kaufman 'the longest suicide note in history'. Labour was, as a result of the events which culminated in the special conference, rendered unelectable. The most immediate consequence was the formation of the SDP, which split the anti-Conservative vote and allowed the Tories near-total dominance of the political landscape for over a decade. These two developments led to the creation of New Labour, as a group around Tony Blair and Gordon Brown realized that unless voters could be persuaded that Labour in the 1990s had almost nothing in common with Labour in the 1980s, the best the party could ever manage would be to sneak into power when voters got fed up with the Conservatives. And the electoral impregnability of New Labour led the so-called Cameroons in the Conservative Party to realize the reverse of that coin: that the Conservatives needed their own shake-up if they were ever to usurp New Labour. It was only when the self-styled 'heir to Blair' took over the party that it was in a position to capitalize on the inadequacies of Labour's doomed Prime Minister, Gordon Brown.

All these developments stem from that one day, 24 January 1981, when Labour formally rejected sanity and embraced lunacy.

The collapse of the 1974–9 Labour government and the consequent Conservative victory in 1979 opened Labour up to a civil war which lasted for almost a decade. But it was at its most poisonous in the immediate post-defeat period. The civil war was fought not just over party policy but also over areas which now seem arcane, such as the precise method for electing the leader. The eventual mechanism, an electoral college in which 40 per cent of the votes were allocated to the trade unions, 30 per cent to the Parliamentary Labour Party and 30 per cent to constituency parties, was a near-total triumph for the Bennites and demonstrated to many of the more moderate members of the party that the game was up.

The day after the conference, David Owen, who had been appointed as a young, dashing Foreign Secretary by

James Callaghan in the previous government, and three other leading Labour politicians, William Rodgers, Shirley Williams and Roy Jenkins, published the so-called Limehouse Declaration, which announced the establishment of a Council for Social Democracy to 'rally all those who are committed to the values, principles and policies of social democracy' and address the need for a 'realignment of British politics'. The result was the creation of the Social Democratic Party, officially launched on 26 March 1981; and with that came the longer-term consequences outlined above.

The Labour government of 1974–9 has become a byword for failure, a physical, political representation of the collapse of Britain in the 1970s. Inflation, unemployment, overweening trade union power, impotent parliamentary power, inefficiency, business collapse, sterling collapse, strikes, power cuts . . . the list is almost endless.

The rot had set in well before Harold Wilson was the unexpected and narrow winner of the first 1974 election. The chaos and strife engendered by the 1973 miners' strike – such as power cuts which led to a national three-day working week – had driven the then Conservative Prime Minister, Edward Heath, to ask the country a simple question in the election: who governs Britain? The answer it gave was equally simple: not you. First in February and then in October 1974 – the second election was called by Wilson to try to gain a working majority – Labour was given charge of the country. And it inherited a mess. Britain was widely said by commentators to be ungovernable and the 1974–9 Labour government seemed little more than an exercise in proving it so. In 1964, 2,277,000 working days were lost to strikes. By 1974 the figure was 700 per cent higher: 14,750,000. Unemployment rose from 2.7 per cent in 1973 to 5.6 per cent in 1979. Inflation was almost 30 per cent in 1975. The ultimate humiliation was the decision by the Cabinet in 1976 – more of a call to the emergency services than a calculated weighing-up of the pros and cons – to call in the International Monetary Fund and borrow vast sums from banks simply to enable the government to stay financially afloat. And in November 1976, immediately after James Callaghan had taken over from Wilson as Prime Minister, a series of by-election defeats caused Labour to lose its tiny majority and, from spring 1977 to October 1978, to be forced to rely on the so-called 'LibLab pact' to avoid defeat in the Commons. (The pact was hailed by the Liberals as a major extension of the party's influence. In reality, it meant little more than ministers giving the odd lift in a government car to their Liberal 'twin'.)

Things were already bad enough for Labour by 1978; but what made electoral defeat a near-certainty was the following Winter of Discontent, which saw tens of thousands of private and public-sector workers down tools and strike – notoriously including grave-diggers, which in one incident led to dead bodies piling up for burial. On 28 March 1970 the government was defeated in a no-confidence vote in the House of Commons and then turfed out of office in the consequent election on 3 May, with a 5.2 per cent swing to Mrs Thatcher's Conservatives.

But if the country was in chaos in 1979, the Labour

Party seemed to lie in ruins. Apart from the 1974–9 Cabinet, it would have been difficult to find a living soul who believed that the government had been anything other than a disaster, both for Labour and for the country – and there were not even many of the former Cabinet ministers who found much to praise about their time in office. The 1964–70 Labour government had been, at best, a great disappointment. It seemed that Labour was simply not up to holding office. But from one viewpoint there was a particular reason for the party's failure: betrayal. From the perspective of the left of the Labour Party, the party in government did not merely sell out to the system but actively betrayed socialism, with the IMF loan and the parallel public spending cuts as the ultimate example of that betrayal. In February 1974, after all, the party's manifesto had pledged to 'take shipbuilding, ship repairing and marine engineering into public ownership and control. But we shall not confine the extension of the public sector to the loss-making and subsidized industries. We shall also take over profitable sections of individual firms in those industries where a public holding is essential to enable the government to control prices, stimulate investment, encourage exports, create employment, protect workers and companies and to plan the national economy in the national interest.'

In the fifteen years to 1979, Labour had been in power for all but four years. And yet, despite the manifesto, Britain was still much as it had been before Labour took office. We were a nuclear power. We were in NATO. We had a mixed economy. Even when a National Plan had been introduced in 1965 it had died a death. And where

Labour, of all parties, ought to have been at its strongest, unemployment had hit working people. The very purpose – and one reflected in the name – of the Labour Party was supposed to be full employment and protecting the welfare of working people. It had failed, miserably. So bad was this particular betrayal that the Conservatives were able to strike electoral gold with their now famous 'Labour Isn't Working' poster, with the slogan written in front of a queue of the unemployed.

Added to all this, with still more profound consequences for the future, was the fact of British membership of the Common Market, as it was then known. The European Economic Community cut right across party lines, with a large number of Conservatives sharing the view of many on the left of the Labour Party that Europe was a foreign entanglement too many – a dangerous attack on national sovereignty and, as the latter saw it, a 'Bankers' Ramp'. Middle-of-the-road, 'One Nation' Conservatives, however, had a Europhilia matched only by the right wing of the Labour Party.

In 1971, when Heath put before Parliament the terms for British entry, the cross-party divides were made clear to all when the majority of the Labour Party, including the leader, Wilson, voted against but sixty-nine Labour MPs, including Roy Jenkins and Shirley Williams, voted with the Conservative government in favour of entry. This event was seismic enough on its own terms, but it also had deep long-term consequences. Tony Benn wrote in his diary in January 1981, after his triumph at the Wembley special conference, that '. . . the Campaign for Labour Party Democracy [the main left-wing organizing faction within the Labour Party in the 1970s and 80s] was really triggered off by the votes of certain Labour MPs in 1971 against a three-line whip, to give Heath the majority needed to take us into the Common Market'.[1] When Labour returned to office in 1974, the politically agile Wilson dealt with this seemingly insuperable internal split by holding an unprecedented referendum on membership of the EEC and allowing his Cabinet to vote either way. Most Labour MPs fought alongside most Conservatives in favour of remaining members but the 'no' campaign also saw the likes of Tony Benn campaigning with Enoch Powell. The issue of Europe was to have huge political consequences over the next thirty years. Even in 2009 it continues to be politically toxic.

The all-encompassing Labour failures appeared to destroy the basis of the tacit bargain which had kept the party together for so long: that even though party activists might be from the left, only the right wing of the party could win elections, given the views of floating voters. But it seemed that even the right could no longer lay claim to electoral appeal or competence. The party's record in power, with right-wing Labour governments, was abysmal and it had just suffered the worst reversal of fortune of any major party since 1945. The right's version had been tried and had failed, materially and electorally. How, the left asked, could it do any worse?

Activists had protested and campaigned against the behaviour of the Labour government but in the end had been powerless to stop the Cabinet deciding to act in government as it saw fit. In opposition, however, it was not the Cabinet which dictated terms to an impotent party:

there was no Cabinet. There were simply former ministers tarred with cataclysmic defeat – and activists no longer prepared to accept that others should dictate policy.

Indeed, the very complexion of the party was changing. Defeat was too much for many older members, who were not ideologues but were instead driven by a decent concern to improve the lot of their fellow man. Labour's woeful failure meant that there seemed little point in remaining party members. In 1964, the party had 830,000 individual members. By 1979, it had less than 300,000.[2] The older, traditional members had left, leaving behind them the more ideologically driven, who in turn recruited more members like themselves. Added to those was an entirely new group – entryists from organizations (in reality, other parties) such as the Militant Tendency. Within a very short time, the party membership's default position shifted to the more extreme left, just as the right's claims to competence and efficacy were shot through by its record in government.

The left had already made headway in the third wing of the party, the unions. Traditionally, trade union leaders had been right-wing political bruisers, weighing in at party conferences to smash activists' hopes with the weight of their block vote. But committed left-wingers within the unions were no longer backing but destroying Labour governments. As the Cabinet started to 'interfere' (as the unions saw it) in industrial relations law, starting with Barbara Castle's *In Place of Strife* proposals under Wilson in 1969, so the unions decided to become more involved in Labour Party policy-making. And so the appeal of left-wing leaders grew – standing up, as they saw it, for unions' rights. Men such as Jack Jones of the TGWU and Hugh Scanlon of the AEU did much damage in the Winter of Discontent; in opposition they were equally destructive.

The unions also started to make themselves felt in local constituencies. Traditionally, unions had effective control of some local constituency parties but exercised that control when selecting parliamentary candidates not by pushing for ideological purity but by deciding whether or not a prospective candidate would do a good job, or selecting as a Buggins' turn reward for loyal service. As 'betrayal' started to be the watchword of many members, however, they became more conscious of the need to select candidates who would implement the policies they wanted. It soon became almost impossible for a prospective Labour MP to win selection without at least pretending to be from the left. After the 1979 election, with many long-serving right-wing Labour MPs having lost their seats, the complexion of the Parliamentary Labour Party (PLP) started to shift. The same shift occurred in the party's governing body, the National Executive Committee. Even by 1974 only one MP not from the left – Denis Healey – was elected to the NEC by Labour Party members, and only one – Shirley Williams – to the party's women's section. By 1979, Healey had been voted off. The right could usually secure no more than four of the NEC's twenty-nine votes. In power, this mattered little. It caused tensions but the NEC could not order the Cabinet around. In opposition, it could not have mattered more. The NEC determined party affairs and the left had total control.

Pressure to reform Labour's constitution had been building since the end of the 1964–70 government. By the mid-1970s, the left had organized itself and was able to capitalize on the seeming confirmation by the 1974–9 government that Labour in government could not be trusted to implement socialism. So the answer was to change the people themselves, selecting genuine socialists as MPs, rather than those who made up the existing PLP, who were generally viewed as right-wing careerists and time-servers. That meant changes to the party's constitution. Existing MPs should be made to submit to reselection before every election, so activists would have the power to keep them in line. Unions and constituency party executives should be able to choose the party leader, rather than simply the PLP, through a vote at the party conference. And the NEC rather than the party leader should write the manifesto so as to avoid any future leader repeating Wilson's 1974 veto of the NEC's plan to include the nationalization of 'twenty-five major companies' as a manifesto pledge. These three demands, which were pushed for by the Campaign for Labour Party Democracy (CLPD), the left's umbrella organization, became the focus of the battles which ripped Labour apart in the 1980s and which transformed British politics, handing victory to Mrs Thatcher, creating New Labour and spawning the Cameroons.

The left was rampant, the right clueless and defensive. It had neither the numbers, the organization nor the personalities to fight. Yes, it had – with the hugely important exception of Tony Benn – most of the major Labour political figures. But for all the internecine battles on the left –

famously parodied by the *Life of Brian* sketch about the passionate differences between the People's Front of Judea and the Judean People's Front – the right, too, was riven by personality clashes. Many simply hated each other. Denis Healey, for instance, described David Owen thus: 'When he was born, all the good fairies gave him every virtue: "You'll be beautiful, you'll be intelligent, you'll have charm and charisma." And the bad fairy came along and tapped him on the shoulder and said, "But you'll be a shit." That was his trouble.'[3] Even if they had all banded together to fight, fight and fight again for the party they loved, they would have had to bow to the sheer numerical strength of the left. But, instead, they split – both within the party, into ineffectual groups such as Solidarity and the Campaign for Labour Victory, and outside the party, into the SDP. Benn and the left were unstoppable. Events were moulded and driven by the left and the right was only ever able to scurry around seeking accommodation where possible, and less explosive terms of surrender where not.

The SDP was never pre-ordained. Even its founders were not sure what they wanted to do until close to its launch. The first public notion that such a party was in the offing came when Roy Jenkins, a former Labour Home Secretary, Chancellor and Deputy Leader, who had gone to Brussels as President of the European Commission, delivered the BBC's Dimbleby Lecture on 22 November 1979. Entitled 'Home Thoughts from Abroad', it condemned 'the constricting rigidity – almost the tyranny – of the present party system'.[4] As for the Labour Party's civil war: 'The response to such a situation, in my view, should not be to slog through an unending war of attrition . . .

100

but to break out and mount a battle of movement on new higher ground.' Jenkins himself summed up the response to the lecture: 'It was like a Victorian lady showing her ankle.'[5] At this stage, however, the 'Gang of Three' (Owen, Williams and Rodgers) were still within the Labour Party, fighting to preserve a measure of sense. They had not, yet, decided that the game was up. Even Roy Jenkins did not know where, practically, to turn to break the mould of British politics.

Within a year of the party's defeat in 1979, the electorate was making clear its feelings about the direction in which Labour was travelling and showing that the right's traditional argument about electoral necessity had genuine merit. In January 1980 an opinion poll in *The Times* found that 60 per cent of voters agreed with the statement that 'The Labour Party is moving too much to the left for my liking'.[6] The 1979 party conference had seen votes in favour of mandatory reselection and NEC control of the manifesto as well as a vote to 'reconsider' EEC membership. And Tony Benn topped the poll for the NEC. Not surprisingly, and accurately, the CLPD secretary called it a 'breakthrough year'.[7]

The left had a clear leader, Benn. The right, however, was full of leaders and thus devoid of real leadership. One man, however, who had previously been dismissed as an over-promoted lightweight when he became Foreign Secretary at thirty-eight, started to carry the fight to the left, delivering a series of clearly argued speeches and highlighting the damaging consequences for the Labour Party if the left had its way. David Owen had enjoyed a meteoric career, elected an MP at twenty-eight and made Foreign

Secretary within a decade of his entry to the Commons. Owen argued initially that 'the most foolish course now for those who are determined to swing the Labour Party to sensible socialism would be to abandon the struggle within the Labour Party, to talk of founding new parties, to break out from the Labour Party'.[8] But he soon changed his mind. At a special party conference held in May 1980, he realized that the party had grown so out of control, so rancorous and so divorced from reality that it might well be beyond salvation. As the historians of the SDP describe it: 'Owen sat at the back of the hall throughout all this, his gorge rising. Apart from Callaghan, no one defended the PLP, no one defended the Labour government, and no one defended, in particular, the Labour government's record in foreign affairs. Owen had not originally intended to speak, but finally he could stand it no longer. He strode to the rostrum and 'spoke from the gut'.[9] He was booed, jeered, hissed and shouted at. The chairman had to tell the conference that: 'This is a serious conference and it is not a shouting match'.[10] At that moment, Owen realized that things were far worse than he had fully comprehended. Six days later he was meeting with Shirley Williams and Bill Rodgers and the so-called Gang of Three was born. As a first step, they agreed to issue a joint statement on Europe, attacking a call by a group of Labour MPs for the UK to withdraw.

1980 saw further argument – battle, more like – over the constitutional changes demanded by the left. That year's party conference was almost comically poisonous, with every moment of TV exposure serving only to show that Labour was beyond the realms of acceptance as

a mainstream party. It began with a piece of dema-
goguery from Tony Benn, demanding that the next
Labour government introduce an Industry Act to enable
full-on nationalization, control of capital movements and
union representation on company boards; withdraw from
the EEC; and then create a thousand peers to take control of the House of Lords: 'Comrades. This is the very
least we must do.'[11] And all within a month of Labour
taking office. He sounded not so much ambitious as
simply mad. But the most significant occurrence was the
decision to hold a special conference to deal with the
issue of election of the party leader – the fateful conference of 24 January 1981, which changed the course of
British history and also, ironically, finally killed off any
chance of socialism taking hold in either Britain or the
Labour Party.

Immediately after the conference, Callaghan resigned as
leader. At that stage, the choice of his successor still rested
with the PLP – the principle of the electoral college had
been agreed but not its details. Benn declined to stand,
arguing that any leader elected solely by the PLP would
be illegitimate, so the election came down, effectively, to
Denis Healey versus Michael Foot. Healey fought an odd
campaign, seeming to behave as if he felt he deserved to
win and should not have to demean himself by chasing
votes. Worse, he acquiesced in the left's arguments, refusing to condemn either their constitutional demands (such
as mandatory reselection and the electoral college) or
their still more extreme policy demands (such as unilateral
disarmament, which he clearly despised). The upshot was
not merely that Foot won (by 139 votes to 129) but that

the forces of the centre and right in the party were still more dispirited. Even if he had lost, Healey might nonetheless have given heart to the right if he had fought a spirited campaign. Instead, his lethargy and cowardice made a bad situation worse and ratcheted up the likelihood of a split as his natural supporters despaired at the lack of leadership or fight. Healey gave people no reason to stay. Had he fought, he would have given them less reason to leave. (There had been a similar occurrence when Roy Hattersley, a politician who huffed and puffed but was ultimately a gutless representative of social democracy within the party, persuaded the Shadow Cabinet during the leadership ballot to accept an electoral college of 55 per cent PLP and 45 per cent Constituency Labour Parties and trade unions. This was, for Owen, yet more evidence of the spinelessness of his Shadow Cabinet colleagues and the inevitability of continuous defeat, even when – as in the Shadow Cabinet – the left was in a minority.)

The press was not slow to pick up on what all this might mean. As Hugo Young put it in the *Sunday Times*: 'A new party is in the making before our very eyes.'[12] As sometimes happens in politics, a mood began to take hold, a change in the assumptions on which politics and politicians are based. Over that Christmas, the expectation emerged that something would indeed change. As Crewe and King put it in their history of the SDP: 'Sometime over the 1980 Christmas break, 24 January 1981 ceased to be any date and became the critical date. An opinion poll at the time also suggested that, if Jenkins and the Gang of Three were going to act at all, they should be getting on with it: it showed a social-democratic-Liberal alliance leading both of the other parties.'[13]

The day itself was even more of a disaster for the Labour Party than had been predicted. Shirley Williams was on the platform as an NEC member; David Owen and Bill Rodgers attended as MPs. Roy Jenkins watched on TV at home. Michael Foot pleaded with the party to give the PLP half the votes in the new electoral college; the NEC recommended a third to the PLP, a third to the CLPs and a third to the unions. But the conference voted – the unions voted, in other words – by 3,375,000 votes to 2,865,000 for the unions to have 40 per cent and the CLPs and PLP 30 per cent each. There was a loud gasp as the result was declared. According to Crewe and King: 'The events at Wembley were bound to do Labour the maximum amount of damage. More important, the breakaway would now be widely seen as inevitable and justified – and would attract additional support.'[14]

The next day, exactly that happened. Nine Labour MPs, plus Owen, Rodgers and the former MP, Williams, made public their support for the 'Council for Social Democracy', the precursor to the SDP. The statement setting up the council was dubbed the Limehouse Declaration, after Owen's Docklands house from which it was issued. As the statement explained:

> The calamitous outcome of the Labour Party Wembley conference demands a new start in British politics. A handful of trade union leaders can now dictate the choice of a future Prime Minister. The conference disaster is the culmination of a long process by which the

Labour Party has moved steadily away from its roots in the people of this country and its commitment to parliamentary government. We propose to set up a Council for Social Democracy. Our intention is to rally all those who are committed to the values, principles and policies of social democracy. We seek to reverse Britain's economic decline. We want to create an open, classless and more equal society, one which rejects ugly prejudices based upon sex, race or religion.

A first list of those who have agreed to support the Council will be announced at an early date. Some of them have been actively and continuously engaged in Labour politics. A few were so engaged in the past, but have ceased to be so recently. Others have been mainly active in spheres outside party politics. We do not believe the fight for the ideals we share and for the recovery of our country should be limited only to politicians. It will need the support of men and women in all parts of our society. The Council will represent a coming together of several streams: politicians who recognise that the drift towards extremism in the Labour Party is not compatible with the democratic traditions of the party they joined and those from outside politics who believe that the country cannot be saved without changing the sterile and rigid framework into which the British political system has increasingly fallen in the last two decades . . .We recognise that for those people who have given much of their lives to the Labour Party, the choice that lies ahead will be deeply painful. But we believe that the need for a realignment of British politics must now be faced.

The media frenzy which followed was unprecedented. The new party had not even been launched but was already being hailed as the saviour of British democracy. On 5 February, a full-page advert signed by a hundred worthies in the *Guardian* – the house journal of the nascent party – received over 25,000 replies. Postal deliveries to the party's makeshift offices brought cash, at the rate of £1000 a day.[15] Opinion polls showed a massive lead for the proposed party. A typical poll, by NOP, recorded 46 per cent support, with just 27 per cent for Labour and 25 per cent for the Conservatives. Michael Foot did his best to halt the thing in its tracks, meeting and pleading with Owen, Rodgers and Williams in his Commons office on 2 February, but to no avail. The dice had already been thrown after the events of 24 January. On 26 March, the SDP was born.

Its impact was immediate. Twenty-eight sitting Labour MPs and one Conservative joined the new party. Jenkins and Williams won thumping by-election victories in Glasgow Hillhead and Crosby respectively and joined them in the Commons. Jenkins had previously fought and narrowly lost a by-election in July 1981, in the safe Labour seat of Warrington. It was, he said, his 'first defeat, but by far [his] greatest victory'. So great was the SDP–Liberal Alliance's impact at by-elections, and so high were its poll ratings, that Liberal leader David Steel felt able to conclude his speech to the 1981 Liberal Party conference with the instruction to delegates to: 'Go back to your constituencies, and prepare for government.' The momentum seemed to be maintained in 1983 when Labour lost Bermondsey, one of its ten safest seats, to the Liberal candidate, Simon Hughes. Hindsight, however, shows that however scintillating the alliance's success in winning by-elections might have been, its real impact was not in putting a new party into government; it was first in entrenching the Conservatives' hold on power, and then ensuring that Labour was turned into an electable party once again.

However badly the Conservatives had been polling at the time of the SDP's launch, victory in the Falklands in June 1982 was a springboard for recovery. In the 1983 election the SDP–Liberal Alliance won 25 per cent of the vote – a huge improvement on the Liberals' 13 per cent in 1979 but nothing like as impressive as the early polls had appeared to promise. Labour received 27.6 per cent, show-ing that even at its worst – with the longest suicide note in history as its manifesto – it could still count on a basic core vote. This the alliance could not touch. Not that Labour could ever have won in 1983 – the Conservatives received 42.4 per cent of the votes, not least out of a decisive anti-Labour sentiment. With the alliance's own 25.4 per cent of the vote taken (in part) from Labour, the Conservatives' House of Commons majority was 144.

The British electorate has a habit of getting to the heart of the matter. When it really matters – in 1979 and 1997, for example – it has made clear where it thinks the coun-try needs to be taken. As the SDP's history shows, third parties can have a real impact but only as catalysts for change within the two main parties. And as the history of British politics after 24 January 1981 shows, it is in equi-librium when a moderately left-of-centre party is opposed by a moderately right-of-centre party. The only plausible reading of the past three decades is that voters' default preference is for a sensible social democrat government and that they turn to the Conservatives only when the Labour Party presents itself as unelectable. (The same phenomenon appears to be in play in 2009.) There was no mass embrace of Thatcherism in the 1980s. But there was a collapse in support for Labour with the unilateralist, isolationist party managing just 27.6 per cent of the vote in 1983 and the barely improved version getting 30.8 per cent in 1987. Once it started to move to the centre, Labour re-entered the fray. Had it gone into the 1992 election with a leader seen by voters as fit to be Prime Minister, rather than with Neil Kinnock, then it might have closed the gap still more, but it still managed to reduce the Conservatives' majority to 21. As for the elections of 1997, 2001 and 2005: if the Conservatives had been led by a combination of Solomon, Aristotle, Churchill and Bobby Moore the party would still have been crushed. Under Blair, Labour was not merely electable; as a modern social democrat party, it really was – in 1997 – the political wing of the British people. And so those election results reflected the voters' default preference. The Conservatives did not have a prayer.

But for all that Labour had changed, New Labour was never more than a tiny coterie within the party, a revolutionary cell which seized control with Tony Blair's election as leader in July 1994. It had just two fully paid-up members in Parliament, Messrs Blair and Mandelson, joined by the one other true believer, polling guru Philip Gould, and then Blair's press secretary, Alastair Campbell, and the Shadow Chancellor, Gordon Brown, a tax-and-spend socialist who saw the tactical advantage which New Labour provided. This simple fact explains almost every aspect of Mr Blair's behaviour in government. Mr Blair behaved, like all coup leaders, as if his control of the Labour Party could end tomorrow, mixing paranoia with ruthlessness and, at times, despair. So he would always do everything possible to shore up his position outside the party, and that often meant snuggling up to the many wealthy businessmen keen to play ball. New Labour was not merely obsequious to business; it revered businessmen as if they were direct descendants of Zeus and Aristotle rolled into one. (For much of the 1990s I worked as a New Labour policy wonk. The one guaranteed way to ensure support from the Blairites was to mention that business supported or, even better, was involved in a policy.)

Up until July 2000, New Labour was clearly running the show. By sticking to the Conservatives' spending plans, which Labour pledged to do in opposition as a convincing demonstration of its fitness to be given charge of the economy, it seemed to be driven by Tony Blair's promise in the 1997 election that New Labour would be 'wise spenders, not big spenders'. New Labour was different from 'tax-and-spend' Labour; it realized that it was the quality of spending which mattered, rather than its size.

But one key figure had never been a true New Labour believer: Gordon Brown. The Chancellor knew quite well that 'tax and spend' was politically impossible until the electorate was convinced that Labour could be trusted on the economy. But once that trust had been gained, then he could start to do the real job of a Labour Chancellor –

spending money. And that was his governing credo from 2000 until becoming Prime Minister in 2007 – raising taxes to finance a public spending spree and borrowing to spend even more. By 2001, the party had an election message of 'Tory tax cuts versus Labour public spending' – about as far from a New Labour message as it was possible to get. New Labour was about killing off the idea that Labour was a tax-and-spend party. Real Labour – as the government became – was about reverting to type.

As the disastrous events of 2008 (which sprang from the Midas-in-reverse touch of Gordon Brown) showed, the New Labour strategy was not merely politically savvy; it was also economically sensible. The spend, spend, spend approach had already been tried by a Labour government – in 1974. And we have already seen how that fared. So it should have come as no surprise when the incompetence of the Chancellor, Gordon Brown, the most overrated politician of the past thirty years – a prosaic thinker, a dreadful strategist, a terrible speaker and, just to ensure his unsuitability as a leader, a man with a personality which repels rather than attracts – meant that Mr Brown was left, somewhat appropriately, to deal as Prime Minister with the consequences of his poisoned legacy. And he couldn't, for the simple reason that he was not up to the job. An over-rated, overpromoted, overspun political hack.

What exacerbated Mr Brown's problems was that he was faced, as no Labour leader since Neil Kinnock had been, with a Conservative leader aware of the realities of politics and with the strategy to turn that to his advantage. Blair versus John Major, Blair versus William Hague, Blair versus Iain Duncan Smith and Blair versus Michael

Howard were fought as the centre versus the right. Not surprisingly, the centre won. It always has. Even Baroness Thatcher won her three elections because she was seen as being closest to the centre, in contrast to a left-wing Labour Party. Cameron saw clearly that the Conservative Party's previous tactics were a waste of time and effort. Conservative support amongst social groups A and B – professionals – had fallen in every election since 1992 (it fell a further 2 per cent in 2005 from the already record low of 2001) and after 2005 stood at 37 per cent. If the party were ever to win again, it would have to secure their support. Yet its unrelenting focus in 2005 on issues such as immigration, and the image of the party to which that contributed, might have been calculated to dissuade ABs from lending their support to the party. ABs were once, and had to be once more if the party were ever to win again, natural Tory voters. But, as the former Director of the Conservative Research Department, Daniel Finkelstein, writes:

The accusation that the party has been running core vote campaigns is quite wrong. The core of Tory support – the wealthy, the educated, the successful – has been turning away from the party. And instead of trying to lure those people back, Conservatives have been trying to replace them with other people, people with less 'advanced' social views. It's not been a core vote strategy, it's been a transfusion strategy . . . It has not worked. It will not work. And not just because the number of AB voters is growing and turns out in higher proportions. It's also because AB views rub off on

112

everyone else. The Tory party can try to change the opinions of AB voters. Or it can accept those opinions and adapt to them. What it cannot do is ignore them. The thing about the chattering classes, you see, is that they chatter.[16]

Far from reaching out and winning support, the party's concentration on themes such as immigration and asylum – essentially shouting 'Bloody foreigners' like Alf Garnett and assuming that the electorate would nod in agreement – could not have been more explicit in sending out the message to those critical As and Bs that the Conservative Party was not thinking remotely what they were thinking.

Part of Tony Blair's political genius was that, in rescuing a decaying party, he did not seek to pretend he was starting from Year Zero. He kept hold of what the public liked about Labour – its concern for social justice – but ditched what it didn't like – economic incompetence and hatred of success. He replaced them with an acceptance of the market to demonstrate that the party now understood the way the world worked. That was one of the key lessons learned by Cameron: yes, a party must always play to its strengths; but it must also make clear that when the public says it is wrong about an issue, the response should not be to demand a new public but to listen and adapt. As Brown's nemesis, Cameron had to do what all previous election winners have done, Labour or Conservative: position his or her party to be seen as fighting from the centre, in contrast to the opponent. To push Brown towards almost certain defeat, Cameron learned from the master, Blair. Blair learned from the splits and fractures of the 1980s. And the splits and fractures took root after the Labour Party special conference on 24 January 1981.

6

THE MONARCHY

15 June 1987

On 15 June 1987, the monarchy of British tradition died. No Act of Parliament was passed. No public campaign took place. No member of the royal family even suffered an illness. But from that day onwards, the game was up for the Windsors. Instead of deference, there was ridicule. Instead of dignity, there was tawdriness.

The staging of *The Grand Knockout Tournament*, to give it its official name – although it was known to everyone at the time and since as *It's a Royal Knockout* – was GUBU: grotesque, unbelievable, bizarre and unprecedented, to use the acronym coined in an entirely different context by the Irish writer Conor Cruise O'Brien.

It's a Knockout was an entertainment show on the BBC which ran from 1966 to 1982 (although it was revived to little impact on Channel Five from 1999 to 2001). Teams representing British towns competed against each other in bizarre games, which mostly involved throwing or avoiding water, large inflated objects, grease and other mildly unpleasant weapons, whilst dressed in over-the-top costumes. Based on the continental series *Jeux Sans Frontières*, it was popular evening viewing, as competitors made fools of themselves in good spirits. But although at its peak in the mid-1970s it drew audiences of 19 million, by the end of its run on BBC1 its viewing figures were a shadow of its former popularity. What was funny and popular in the 1970s no longer appealed to a 1980s audience.

Unbeknownst to most viewers, one of the programme's biggest fans was Prince Edward, Queen Elizabeth's youngest son, who would apparently make every effort to watch. The prince was perhaps the least popularly regarded of all the Queen's children, in part because he seemed to have had a high opinion of himself from an early age. As the *Guardian* writer Andy Beckett wrote in a profile of him: 'In 1969, in the pioneering official documentary *Royal Family*, among the would-be intimate scenes of the Queen visiting a corner shop and Prince Philip standing over a barbecue, Edward was an attention-seeking presence: demanding ice cream, clambering on to the roof of the parked family Range Rover. Television critics remarked on his precocious on-camera confidence.'[1] And so, casting around for something to do after leaving university and a short spell in the Royal Marines, the 23-year-old prince decided that he would become a TV producer. As such, he conceived the idea of a one-off revival of his much-loved programme. Fine, if rather passé, one might have thought. But Edward had a particular idea for the special edition. The teams would not represent towns; they would represent medieval knights. And who better to do that than members of his own royal family.

With one bound he would establish himself as the serious player he deserved to be. In one fell swoop he would change the public's perception of him from a leech on the public purse, a prince with no purpose, to a self-sufficient, creative and well-respected media professional. Of course the prince's definition of self-sufficiency was rather different from most people's: the central plank of his plan was to use his royal status to advance his career, luring his siblings and showbiz names to take part in the programme. But that is by the by, and because it did not detain the prince it need not detain us.

Edward assembled a committee to organize the project, including his friends Tim Hastie-Smith, James Baker, Abel Hadden and the photographer Jayne Fincher. Ms Fincher spoke well of his involvement in the project: 'Edward was in charge of everything and what surprised me was what a good leader he was, without being bossy. He was an excellent motivator and good at getting the right people together. What I found particularly fascinating was how artistic he was. He did a lot of sketches himself . . . He was very meticulous even down to the costume details.'[2] That may have been the case. But the event was nonetheless a disaster. Every single aspect was ruinous, with long-term consequences far worse even than the imaginings of those – pretty much everyone who thought about it, in reality – who realized that there could be few more stupid things for an institution which depended on respect and dignity for its very existence to do than participate in a programme designed with the specific intention of inflicting not merely indignity but humiliation on its participants.

At the press conference called to announce the project, the prince promised: 'The games [will be] slightly different from the old *It's a Knockout* . . . We've deliberately kept a sense of decorum.' Once again, the prince's definition of decorum appears to have differed somewhat from most people's. One can only imagine how Prince Edward sold the event to his family. But whether it was through subtle persuasion or whiny pleading, he succeeded – about the only instance in the entire fiasco to which the word success can be applied.

The day itself was cold and wet. On a site built on a field in Staffordshire, there were four teams, each captained by a royal: Edward himself, Princess Anne, and the Duke and Duchess of York. Among the team members were sports stars such as Sunil Gavaskar, Viv Richards, Jackie Stewart, Steve Cram and Gary Lineker, actors including Jenny Agutter, Christopher Reeve and John Travolta, and singers such as Kiri te Kanawa, Cliff Richard and Tom Jones. Each team was sponsored by a charity: the World Wildlife Fund, the International Year of Shelter for the Homeless, Save the Children and the Duke of Edinburgh Award. And, to be fair, the event raised £1 million, thanks to corporate sponsorship. The Prince and Princess of Wales had the sense to steer well clear, having no connection with the event and making no public comment about it before, during or after.

But like all PR disasters, the specifics are blurred in the memory. Contrary to the mythology which has grown up surrounding the event, the captains – the royals themselves –

did not actually take part in the games: the Queen had refused permission for that. They stood at the side, cheering and yelling. But much good that did them – they were and remain tarred by its brush as much as if they had been throwing rotten vegetables and pushing water uphill themselves. One game involved six people dressing up as giant vegetables (two each as potatoes, leeks and onions) and then being chased by opponents to have their costumes removed and thrown into a giant black cauldron. In another, contestants had giant hams thrown at them while trying to cross foam-covered logs and a table on a pool of water. So much for what the Victorian commentator Walter Bagehot referred to as the dignified part of the constitution.

Edward later described the day as 'the event of the year'. The BBC, he said, had 'positively drooled at the idea'. And it had all been his triumph! He was, he said, 'overall producer' for 'easily the largest outside broadcast of the year'. It was 'the most extraordinary day in my life'.[3] Indeed. Not many members of the royal family can lay claim to signalling the beginning of the end of a centuries-old institution.

But as if staging so entirely misconceived an event were not bad enough, Prince Edward also seems to have gone out of his way to ensure as bad a press as possible – not least in banning any media presence beyond the BBC coverage and his photographer friend Jayne Fincher. An arrogant young man with all the privileges and none of the humility befitting his status, he began the press conference after the event with a question: 'Well, what did you think?' The journalists in the room laughed. Piqued that he had not got something akin to a standing ovation, Edward stormed off in a huff, sarcastically thanking those present for their enthusiasm. On its own, the event would have entered legend as a disaster. But Edward's puerile, haughty and conceited behaviour throughout the process, culminating in his walking out of the press conference, made a bad situation a lot worse.

Prince Edward's subsequent career as a TV producer was also based almost entirely on attempting to make money from his royal status. Topics dealt with by his company, Ardent, were typically subjects such as the restoration of Windsor Castle after its fire and English royal warships. Its interviewees comprised royal retainers and family members. One of its earliest programmes was a documentary about Edward VIII. The prince's involvement was par for the course, as Andy Beckett describes:

> During filming, Edward was keen to conduct the interviews himself, although he had little television experience. Despite being its 'joint managing director and head of production', Edward had no formal pre-Ardent qualifications as a television researcher or producer or director, or as a broadcast journalist. Nevertheless, it was arranged one day that he would question, on camera, the only living witness to a notorious meeting between the Duke of Windsor and Hitler. The interview subject was an elderly man who spoke fluent German; whatever had been said at the meeting, which had been the subject of decades of speculation, he had heard every word of it. But when Edward started to question him, in his polite, clipped royal voice, with his characteristic, slightly stiff hand gestures and nods of the head – the usual battle going on between retaining

princely dignity and achieving televisual informality – it gradually became clear that Edward was getting nowhere. He was just circling round the central issue of the infamous meeting. 'Eventually I had to stop the interview,' says Christine Carter, the documentary's producer. 'And I said to Edward and the interviewee, "What did the Duke of Windsor say to Hitler?" Edward said, "Chris, you'd better do this interview."'[4]

The Prince's company survived for nine years. It was a shambles, described by another producer at the time of its collapse as: '[A] sad joke in the industry, really . . . As time has gone on, their incompetence has become more and more obvious. There have been very small examples of vanity TV companies before, but not on this scale. Any company, in any industry, that had burned through that much share capital without making a profit would've been closed down by its investors years ago.'[5] And its behaviour was often as arrogant and unthinking as that of its founder, such as when it was discovered filming Prince William as a student at St Andrews undercover to get footage for a programme it was making for the US, *The A–Z of Royalty*. Prince Edward was forced to apologize to his nephew and to his brother, the Prince of Wales.[6] In 2002, Ardent closed with losses of over £2 million. But whatever Edward's company's losses, the loss to the royal family brought about by the prince's first venture into TV production was incalculable. *It's a Royal Knockout* was the beginning of the end – the moment from which the royal family became forever a laughing stock.

*

It would, of course, be wrong to blame Prince Edward and his programme single-handedly for the end of deference to and respect for royalty. In some ways, *It's a Royal Knockout* was a symptom of the already collapsed image of royalty. One could argue that the rot had set in in 1969, with the BBC fly-on-the-wall documentary *Royal Family* – the first time that royalty had been treated as simply another form of celebrity. Instead of the traditional aloofness and mystery, the documentary revealed the royals as being like any other family – albeit a far more privileged one. From BBQs to tiffs – they had them all.

The family faced a choice. The new age of media and journalism no longer deferred to authority figures, and they had to adapt to this. But how? They could have chosen to make themselves more accessible, more normal, and more down to earth – to become more like the surviving European royal families, such as the so-called 'bicycling monarchs' epitomized by Queen Juliana of the Netherlands. But rather than do this, they became instead precursors to the modern phenomenon of celebrity. The Queen's sister, Princess Margaret, for instance, could have sought recognition for her good works; instead, she became a staple of the diary columns for her partying, drinking and liaison with the socialite Roddy Llewellyn. The family's press advisers sought to create fairy-tale stories, such as the marriage of Princess Anne; but instead all they created was the royal as proto-celebrity, feeding newspapers non-stop stories over the search for a bride for Prince Charles.

For sheer celebrity quotient, of course, none of the royals came close to Charles's first wife. Initially, Diana seemed able to square the role of supportive wife doing good deeds with the increasing public interest in her clothes and her growing celebrity. But by the end of her life, she was treated and reported on as nothing more than a celebrity, albeit the supreme example of the species. Diana may have courted such treatment with her publicity stunts, her carefully chosen dresses, her personal courting of newspaper editors and her determination to use the media to put her version of her life on the record; but the media were able to treat her this way because, after *It's a Royal Knockout*, the notion of royal dignity was risible.

Even the Queen herself came to realize this. 1992 was supposed to be a year of celebration – the fortieth anniversary of her accession to the throne. Instead, it led her to recognize that her family was no longer looked up to; it was, rather, regarded as something of a freak show. Take Sarah Ferguson, the Duchess of York. The word 'dignity' was not in the renowned fun lover's vocabulary. Nor, it seemed from pictures published in January 1992, was the word 'monogamy'. A series of photos did not merely imply that she had been fooling around with a Texan 'friend', Steve Wyatt – it seemed to scream it loud and clear. The Duke and Duchess separated later that month. And then in August that year she was pictured sucking the toes of another American 'friend', John Bryan. 1992 also saw Princess Anne divorcing her first husband, Captain Mark Phillips, accompanied by press reports of love letters to her from a palace staff member and allegations that Captain Phillips had fathered an illegitimate child.

But to cap it all, 1992 was the year the Charles and Diana fairy tale finally collapsed under the weight of the publication of Andrew Morton's supposedly unofficial biography of the Princess of Wales, featuring tales of her misery and suicide attempts and Charles's affair with Camilla Parker-Bowles. Far from being unofficial, it later emerged that Morton's main source was Diana herself, who had supplied him with tape-recorded interviews. The book was explosive. More cringe-making was another set of tapes published in 1993, of risqué phone calls between Charles and Mrs Parker-Bowles in which the heir to the throne explained to his mistress that he would like to 'live inside your trousers', presumably as a tampon. As the former Buckingham Palace aide Charles Anson put it: 'The private lives of the royal family dominated the news more than their public duties. And the function of the monarchy is to perform public duties. It's not to have their private lives played out in public . . . but inevitably that happened.'[7]

But of all the events of 1992, what most stung the Queen was a fire at her favourite home, Windsor Castle, her weekend retreat and the oldest inhabited castle in the world. As if, however, to emphasize how out of touch she had become, she appeared to expect that the taxpayer would deferentially foot the entire restoration bill, estimated then at between £40 and £60 million, tugging its forelock as it handed the money over. In a bygone age, perhaps, when the royals were regarded as a family to look up to rather than how they were then seen: as the archetypal dysfunctional celebrity waste of space. The public reacted with an anger not previously seen directed against the family. The debate which ensued opened up the issue of one of the most galling aspects of the family's behaviour: the royal 'hangers on' – fringe members of the family who nonetheless received money from the civil list. Such was the strength of public feeling that the Prime Minister had to react to stave off further damage to the very survival of the institution of the monarchy. In February 1993, John Major announced to the House of Commons that he had accepted an offer from the Queen to pay tax on her private income and to cut the civil list back to herself, the Duke of Edinburgh and the Queen Mother. She would pay for the activities of the other royals herself. She also confirmed that she would pay 70 per cent of the Windsor Castle restoration costs and open up Buckingham Palace to the public to view. For the first time, for eight weeks in the summer of 1993, the public were allowed in, paying £8 each. Taken alongside the souvenirs sold, this raised £2 million towards the Windsor restoration costs.

As the Queen put it in a speech at the Guildhall on 24 November: '1992 is not a year that I shall look back on with undiluted pleasure . . . It has truly been . . . in the words of one of my more sympathetic chroniclers, my *annus horribilis*.' And then it got worse, with a long-expected confirmation from John Major in the House of Commons: 'It is announced from Buckingham Palace that with regret, the Prince and Princess of Wales have decided to separate.' The royal family no longer behaved with the dignity of royals and was no longer even a family. It was a joke.

But even that has not been sufficient to quieten its single most annoying member, the heir to the throne, who behaves as if his status gives him the right to shoot his mouth off on any of his pet subjects and to expect the rest of us to pay heed to his views, rather than regarding them as the inappropriate rantings of a singularly ignorant bore. Prince Charles's contributions are regular and almost always out of place. The issue is not whether he is right or wrong (although some of his obsessions, such as alternative medicine – more correctly known as quack medicine – are deeply misguided and often dangerous). It is, rather, that the constitutional bargain which allows him his status depends on him keeping his views to himself, as his mother has successfully managed throughout her life.

On the other hand, perhaps we should be grateful to the Prince of Wales. Until he opened his mouth in Abu Dhabi on a trip in February 2007, it is unlikely that many people realized how much healthier it is to eat a Big Mac than one of his own Duchy Originals organic Cornish pasties. On a tour of a diabetes centre, Prince Charles asked a nutritionist: 'Have you got anywhere with McDonald's? Have you tried getting it banned? That is the key.' Typically, his argument revealed more about his own failings than the point he was trying to make. A Duchy Originals organic Cornish pasty has 264 calories per 100g, and a Big Mac only 229 calories; a Duchy Originals pasty has 5.5g of saturated fat, a Big Mac just 4.17g. One has to hand it to the prince. There are not many even in his own family who can manage to be a loudmouth, a danger to the constitution and a buffoon all at the same time.

As he is the heir to the throne, opportunities for displaying such singular qualities arise at will. Whether it's the supposedly deplorable state of modern architecture (a matter of taste), the efficacy of alternative medicine (quackery, not science) or the superiority of organic produce (an assertion with no evidential basis), Prince Charles appears to be a man of limited intellect but with a desperate need to share the product of that intellect with the rest of the country. In May 2008 he was at it again, this time lecturing his countrymen and women on the dangers of deforestation in an interview on the BBC's *Today* programme.

But perhaps Prince Charles is simply preparing himself for the future, not as a monarch but as a pundit. The royal family has, after all, now lost almost all its *raison d'être*. It no longer binds the country together; it divides it. It is no sort of model family, unless, that is, a model of one to be avoided at all costs. Its supposed usefulness as a tourist attraction is based on history. And its behaviour is no better than that of any other celebrity grouping.

7

CRIME

28 January 1953

At 9 a.m. on 28 January 1953, Derek Bentley, a 19-year-old, was hanged at Wandsworth Prison for his part in the murder of PC Sidney Miles. Bentley had been sentenced to death for killing the policeman during a bungled break-in at a warehouse in Croydon. Bentley's co-defendant, Christopher Craig, had fired the shot which killed PC Miles. But because Craig was still legally a juvenile – he was 16 at the time – he escaped the death sentence. Craig might have been the younger man but he was the ringleader; Bentley had the mental age of an 11-year-old and an IQ of 66, he was an epileptic (triggered after a 15-foot fall onto his head from a lorry in 1938) and he was illiterate. He was also in thrall to the younger Craig.

On the night of 2 November 1952, Craig and Bentley had tried to break into a warehouse owned by a confectionery manufacturer. They were spotted by a 9-year-old girl in a house opposite. She told her parents and her father called the police from a phone box. The police arrived quickly and, spotting them, Bentley and Craig hid behind the lift casing on the roof. The first policeman to arrive, Detective Sergeant Frederick Fairfax, climbed up to the roof, spotted Bentley hiding and apprehended him, only for Bentley to break free.

What happened next was the crux of the case. The police said in court that Bentley shouted: 'Let him have it, Chris.' Craig had a gun – a Colt .455 Eley calibre. He had sawn off half the barrel and altered some of the ammunition to fit the gun. On hearing the words, he fired the gun and hit Detective Sergeant Fairfax's shoulder. Injured, the policeman still managed to recapture and arrest Bentley.

More police arrived and the first on the roof was PC Miles. He was immediately killed by a shot to the head from Craig's gun. Craig then ran out of bullets and tried to escape by jumping the ten metres from the roof. His escape was not successful; as he landed he broke his spine and left wrist. He too was then arrested.

The trial of the two men took place between 9 and 11 December 1952 at the Old Bailey, before the Lord Chief Justice, Lord Goddard. One psychiatrist reported that Bentley was borderline retarded but another found that he was not what was held to be a 'feeble-minded person' under the Mental Deficiency Act and that consequently he was fit to plead and stand trial. The doctrine of 'constructive malice' was then still in place, which meant that the *mens rea* (guilty mind) necessary for a murder conviction could still be attributed to a defendant if a death was the result of the commission of another felony, such as robbery or burglary. The case was complicated: Bentley's defence was that he had been under arrest when PC Miles was killed. And both Craig and Bentley also denied that the now infamous words 'Let him have it, Chris' had ever been spoken. The prosecution argued that they had and that they showed a 'common purpose'. Bentley's counsel argued that even if they had been spoken, they would have demonstrated quite the opposite – that Bentley was urging Craig to hand over his weapon. The prosecution was also unable to say how many shots had been fired and by whom, and could not find the fatal bullet; ballistics experts had varying opinions as to whether Craig could have fired deliberately and hit the policeman.

The jury was out for just seventy-five minutes before deciding that both Bentley and Craig were guilty of murder. Craig was ordered to be detained at Her Majesty's pleasure and was released after serving ten years. Bentley was sentenced to the mandatory death sentence. His appeal was heard and dismissed on 13 January 1953. Two hundred MPs protested against the conviction and signed a petition demanding that the Home Secretary, Sir David Maxwell Fyfe, request clemency from the Queen. The campaign for clemency was also supported by much of the media establishment. But Maxwell Fyfe refused; the psychiatric reports, he argued, gave no grounds for clemency.

Bentley's hanging marked the moment at which the abolition of capital punishment became inevitable. The judicial execution of a man for whom capital punishment seemed wholly unsuitable, even to those who accepted that he was guilty, gave those who were already campaigning for its abolition the final and apparently clinching argument in their favour. Over the next ten years the campaign for its abolition grew and grew amongst the establishment. But capital punishment remained overwhelmingly supported by voters, and governments were afraid to allow time for a move which would be so unpopular. Finally, on 21 December 1964, the House of Commons debated abolition. The debate was opened by Sydney Silverman, who had for years been the leading campaigner against capital punishment, describing hanging as 'a grotesque barbarity'. The newly elected Wilson government had surprised everyone with a pledge to allow time for 'a free decision by Parliament on the issue of Capital Punishment'. Free debate it might have been, but it was clear that Silverman's Bill had de facto if not *de jure* government support. As Silverman put it: 'I hope we may count on the neutrality of the government being a benevolent neutrality.' The existing law, the 1957 Homicide Act, was clearly unsatisfactory, a botched compromise which reduced the applicability of hanging to a small number of cases, mainly those involving the police and prison officers, and seemed to offer many MPs the chance effectively to abolish hanging without actually voting to do so.

In the 1964 debate, intellect and moral clarity seemed to lie with the abolitionists, as the defenders of hanging were reduced to apparently wild assertions about the terrible consequences of abolition. Only one defender of the status quo came across as making a reasoned case; a case which, with hindsight, was not merely reasoned but very prescient. Sir Peter Rawlinson, a former Solicitor General, argued: 'Great care is and has been taken by professional criminals to avoid the risk of violence leading to death, because of the difference in the penalty which is paid. I believe we are witnessing an increase in professional crime, and that there is an extension of operations by organised gangs. I fear that the removal of capital punishment from this field of crime would introduce a risk of greater violence, the wider use of guns and greater danger to the public.' Rawlinson's was a utilitarian case; appropriately, J.S. Mill had defended hanging in an earlier debate in the Commons, in April 1868: 'Does fining a criminal show a want of respect for property, or imprisoning him, for personal freedom?'

Capital punishment was finally abolished on 8 November 1965 with the passing of the Murder (Abolition of Death Penalty) Act. Since then, the homicide rate has risen, so that by 1999 it was three times that of 1962.[1]

On 1 April 1997, the Criminal Cases Review Commission referred the Bentley case to the Court of Appeal. The then Lord Chief Justice, Lord Bingham, sitting with Lord Justice Kennedy and Mr Justice Collins, held that Bentley's conviction was 'unsafe'. The summing-up by Lord Goddard 'was such as to deny the appellant that fair trial which is the birthright of every British citizen'. Lord Bingham continued: 'It must be a matter of profound and continuing regret that this mistrial occurred and that the defects we have found were not recognized at the time.' On 30 July 1998, the Court of Appeal set aside Bentley's conviction for murder. Speaking on the day, Christopher Craig said that: 'While I am grateful and relieved about this, I am saddened that it has taken . . . forty-six years for the authorities in this country to admit the truth . . . A day does not go by when I don't think about Derek and now his innocence has been proved with this judgment.'

*

Whatever one's views on the rights or wrongs of judicial execution, capital punishment was not just the sentence for murder. It also underpinned the entire criminal justice system and held many other crimes, and criminals, in check. Capital punishment was the foundation of a system based on personal responsibility and punishment. It rested on each of us being seen as responsible for our own actions. Abolition might have been seen as the morally right thing but it marked the triumph of a view of crime as a treatable social disorder caused by conditions – a view epitomized in the contradictory New Labour slogan 'tough on crime, tough on the causes of crime'. There are no 'causes of crime' beyond criminals.

The upshot of this transformation from a system based on personal responsibility and punishment to one based on the idea of crime as a disease like any other can be seen in a random week's news stories taken from local papers across the UK:

Mrs Brenda Robinson, 66, was arrested for clipping the ear of a boy who had threatened her with a lump of wood and called her a 'xxxxxxx bitch'.

Dyfed Powys Constabulary dispatched an officer at the crack of dawn to interview a local taxpayer who sent a copy of Pastor Martin Niemöller's poem about tyranny to councillors. Stan Rogers was warned he could be prosecuted for harassment.

Hayley Richards was stabbed to death by her Portuguese former lover Hugo Quintas. Although he was known to the police for posing a danger to Miss Richards, they declined to intervene because they did not have an interpreter (even though Quintas spoke fluent English). Then, when Miss Richards called the police to tell them Quintas was in the pub saying he was going to kill her, they refused to act since the two 'spare' male officers were rescuing a dog from a car.

Police are refusing to study CCTV tapes on which criminals are caught in the act because they are 'too busy'.

The police have been instructed to let off offenders with a caution if they commit any one of more than 60 types of crime, ranging from assault to some types of theft, criminal damage and under-age sex. The instructions are contained in a government document sent to forces and released under the Freedom of Information Act. They are designed to reduce inconsistencies that can see offenders in one area escaping with a caution while elsewhere they would be prosecuted for the same offence.

The same mix of incompetence, fatuity and shame is repeated week after week. This is how the criminal justice system has responded to the yob society: by failing in its most basic task of bringing criminals to justice. According to official figures, every year some 30 million people are victims of crime. The Home Office itself estimated in 2002 that there were 60 million crimes a year.[2] The reconviction rate for the 155,000 criminals supervised by the Probation Service is 61 per cent – and that figure only records those who end up being convicted.[3]

The government regularly trumpets the British Crime Survey figures to proclaim its triumph over crime. In July 2008, the official figures showed that there were 5 million recorded crimes in England and Wales, a fall of 9 per cent in the 12 months to March 2008. Except that the official figures didn't say that at all. They said that there were 10.1 million crimes. Why the confusion? Because there are two sets of 'official' figures: crimes recorded by the police and crimes counted by the British Crime Survey. The police figures said there were 5 million crimes and the British Crime Survey figures said there were 10.1 million. Two sets of figures there may be, but they are both misleading. For one thing, the BCS (which is based on 47,000 interviews) is only able to interview people in households which are prepared to allow its people in – and this is a distinct problem in high-crime inner-city areas. Professors Graham Farrell and Ken Pease have, additionally, shown that because the BCS fails to count crimes where the same person is repeatedly the victim of crime, and puts an arbitrary cap of five crimes on the number it counts against any one person, the total number of violent crimes committed against over-16s is likely to be 80 per cent higher than the figure recorded by the BCS.[4] More ridiculously still, they do not include crimes related to illegal drug use, sexual offences, crimes against commercial premises, murder, shoplifting or crimes with a victim less than sixteen years old – in many ways the most worrying area of all. Research shows that one in four children between twelve and sixteen has been a victim of crime, and they are ignored by the BCS.[5]

The Home Office's own private figures estimate that in 2002/3 (the latest available year for such figures) there were 122,008 woundings, 79,457 robberies, 55,858 thefts and 342,507 assaults against 11 to 15-year-olds – a total of 599,830 crimes. An investigation by the Channel 4 *Dispatches* programme in January 2008 found that the number of murder victims under 18 killed by other under-18-year-olds had tripled since 2005: in 2007, there were 37 such murders, compared to 12 in 2005.

Furthermore, the BCS does not include murder or any crime against a victim who is not a permanent UK resident. And it doesn't cover crimes unless they are specifically directed at an individual, so if a school suffers an arson attack or some shops suffer theft then they don't show up on the BCS. There were 2,758,054 crimes against commercial victims (such as vandalism and car thefts) in 2002/3. Using these and other such figures ignored by the BCS, there are some 11 million extra crimes, which when added to the BCS's 12.6 million crimes for 2002/3 shows a total of almost 24 million – and even this does not include sex- or drug-related crimes.[6] One expert calculates (using conservative estimates) that there are 62.7 million offences committed every year.[7] Extrapolating from the figures, we also know that violent crime, as recorded by the number of incidents reported to the police, doubled between 1997 and 2007.[8]

How different things are from a century ago, when, as Jose Harris writes in her social history of pre-First World War Britain:

A very high proportion of Edwardian convicts were in prison for offences that would have been much more lightly treated or wholly disregarded by law enforcers in the late twentieth century. In 1912–13, for example, one quarter of males aged 16 to 21 who were imprisoned in the metropolitan area of London were serving seven-day sentences for offences which included drunkenness, 'playing games in the street', riding a bicycle without lights, gaming, obscene language and sleeping rough. If late twentieth-century standards of policing and sentencing had applied in Edwardian Britain, the prisons would have been virtually empty; conversely, if Edwardian standards were applied in the 1990s then most of the youth of Britain would be in jail.[9]

Not that 1913 was a bad year by any standards: 98,000 offences were recorded. The official figures for recorded crime had remained more or less the same for decades, dipping to 79,000 in 1886 and rising to a peak of 105,000 in 1908 and 1909.[10] By 1931 the figure had started to rise, to 159,000, but it was only in the 1960s that there was a dramatic take-off. By 1971 the level of crime had risen to 1,166,000.

Politicians and those involved in the system dismiss the idea that this reveals anything of note, arguing that more crimes are now reported and there are also now more crimes on the statute book; just as we are repeatedly told that our education system is now at record-breaking achievement levels, so our criminal justice system is better than ever. But even allowing for the problems with official figures and different methodologies, it takes some gall to make that case when the most realistic estimate for the total number of offences committed in a given year is, as we have seen, 62.7 million.

In 1979 there was a one in eleven chance of being a victim of car crime; today three quarters of drivers are victims.[11] In 1979 there was a one in thirty-two chance of suffering a burglary; by 1995 it was one in eleven.[12] In 1957, 340 per 100,000 of the population were convicted of a criminal offence; by 1991 the figure had risen to 1400 – and this at a time when detection rates fell, so even though clear-up rates were falling, ever greater numbers of the population were being convicted of crime.[13] And even on recorded police figures, which dramatically underplay reality, in 2001 there were 6500 robberies in just one London borough, Lambeth; whereas in 1972 there were 8900 robberies in the whole of England and Wales. Indeed, in December 2002 there were 282 robberies in Lambeth – a figure greater than for the entire number of robberies for all of England and Wales in every year bar two between 1918 and 1939.[14] It seems almost impossible to believe that robberies were once so scarce, yet the national annual figure for robbery did not exceed 400 until 1941. As the former probation officer David Fraser writes in his seminal book *A Land Fit for Criminals*:

> When I was a child, the operation of leaving the house was simple and straightforward. You simply went out and closed the door behind you . . . But today it is dogged by fears of predatory burglars who roam through our towns and villages and who commit hundreds of thousands of burglaries every year. As a result, for many,

the once simple act of leaving their house has become a nightmare of anxiety and complicated security routines. Have all the windows and doors been locked? . . . Has the alarm been set? Will anyone leave anything on the doorstep and give away the fact that there is no one in?[15]

Should a criminal be one of the tiny number actually detected (the Audit Commission calculated that even on the underestimated basis of recorded crimes, criminals have only a one in sixteen chance of being caught[16]), let alone punished (over 90 per cent of recorded crimes receive no punishment[17]), then it soon becomes clear that most of his crimes will remain unpunished, as the court will 'take into account' other offences that he might admit to. They are then added to his file as little more than punctuation for his record.

So it is no wonder that the police now teach us how to accept victimhood, as if putting paid to the crime which causes it were far too ambitious a task. Neighbourhood Watch asks us to be vigilant but also bombards us with messages about Victim Support. Millions of pounds are spent telling us not to leave our property in the sight of thieves. Notices at railway stations warn us that thieves are operating and we should be extra-careful; adverts tell us not to be so stupid as to speak into mobile phones as we walk home. Theft is treated as if it were rain – unavoidable and something to be lived through. One writer records the experience of a foreign student in London, briefed by a policewoman on how to keep safe:

Her first question was to the women, 'How many of you brought Mace?' Three girls raised their hands. She told us we couldn't use it, shouldn't even carry it, it was illegal. Had any of us brought any other type of weapon, such as a knife? Several of the men in our group indicated that they carried pocket knives. She told us to leave them at home too. Then she instructed us on how to properly be a victim. If we were attacked, we were to assume a defensive posture, such as raising our hands to block an attack. The reason (and she spelled it out in no uncertain terms) was that if a witness saw the incident and we were to attempt to defend ourselves by fighting back, the witness would be unable to tell who the aggressor was. However, if we rolled up in a ball, it would be quite clear who the victim was.[18]

And God help us if we refuse to accept victimhood and fight back. The old axiom of *ex turpi causa non oritur actio* (no claim may arise out of an evil action) now has no standing. In 1988, retired miner Ted Newbery was sleeping in his allotment shed, fed up as a result of repeated attacks on it by hooligans. The sound of two men breaking in woke him; one shouted out, 'If you're in there, we're having you.' Mr Newbery had a shotgun poked through a hole in the door, and fired it. One of the men, Mark Revill, was hit in the arm and chest. Revill pleaded guilty to his crimes. But not only was Mr Newbery prosecuted – although acquitted by the jury – he was then sued by Revill for damages and ordered to pay £4000. There have since been innumerable cases of people defending themselves who are then prosecuted for using what judges and the prosecuting authorities deem to be excessive force. Better, they imply, to roll over and take what is coming to you.

Even if the criminal is punished, that has now itself become a very loose concept. Home Office figures show that of the 1,468,900 sentences passed in 1998 in England and Wales, only 6.8 per cent led to imprisonment. Between 1981 and 1995 the number of convicted burglars sent to prison fell from 0.78 per cent to 0.22 per cent. At the same time, burglary rates doubled from 40.9 per 1000 households to 82.9. Burglars were 5 times more likely to be imprisoned in 1981 than they are today.[19] Indeed, between 1998 and 2002 just 6 mandatory sentences for burglary were handed out,[20] despite there being 402,984 recorded domestic burglaries.[21]

Knife crime presents an even starker picture. Police figures, which are notorious for underestimating crime, show that almost 60 people are stabbed or mugged at knife-point every day. Data from 33 of the 43 police forces in England and Wales, covering more than four fifths of the population, shows that 20,803 serious knife crimes (murders, stabbings where blood is spilt and knife-point muggings) were recorded in the year to March 2008 – 56 per day. Adding those forces which did not provide figures along with Scotland and Northern Ireland would, of course, make for an even larger total. And if less serious crimes such as threats or illegal possession were included, the figures would be much higher.[22]

In the first six months of 2008 there were twenty-eight teenage murders, prompting a flood of suggestions as to how to deal with the epidemic which seems to have infected our streets. Yet for all the analysis that was offered and the policy ideas suggested, one basic point was forgotten. We have yet to try properly using the laws already on the statute book, let alone giving appropriate punishments to those found in possession of knives. Over the past decade, the number of convictions for carrying a knife has risen from 3360 in 1997 to 6314 in 2006. Of those convicted in 1997, 482 were teenagers, rising in 2006 to 1256. That near-trebling in the number of teenagers convicted is bad enough. Worse, however, is that surveys show that around one in five teenagers says today that they carry a knife with them. Given the rapid development of a teenage culture in which carrying a knife is seen as normal, not to say essential for self-defence, it is understandable that there have been regular calls to toughen the relevant laws. The current maximum sentence for knife-carrying is two years, or four years if the knife is carried to school. But since we do not enforce the existing laws properly, it is fatuous to suggest that tougher maximum penalties would serve any useful purpose. They would be ignored, just like the existing maximum penalties. In 2006, just 9 of the 6314 people convicted for carrying a knife were handed down a maximum sentence. Most were simply given a caution. And it is a near-certainty that not one of those nine criminals – 0.14 per cent of those convicted – will actually have served the full sentence they were given. Despite the penalties available, the criminal authorities treat this potentially deadly crime as an infringement of the law akin to pilfering an apple from a grocer.

Judges simply refuse to accept that prison is appropriate. And yet all the evidence shows that prison works – at least for keeping criminals off the street – and non-custodial sentences simply do not. The reconviction rate for criminals supervised by the probation service is over 60 per cent, but that figure of course represents only those reoffenders who are actually caught – and we saw above that the detection rate is just 5.5 per cent.[23] The repeat offending of the 155,000 criminals under the probation service's 'control' leads to millions of further crimes being committed – crimes which would not have happened if they were in prison. In 1998, for example, offenders under the supervision of the probation service committed 56 murders and attempted murders, 20 manslaughters, 33 rapes, 5 attempted rapes and 13 arsons with intent to endanger life.[24]

As for the supposed rigorous supervision: the National Standards for Offender Supervision are simply risible. The offender should attend a minimum of 12 appointments with the supervising officer in the first 3 months of an order; 6 in the next 3 months; and then 1 monthly. As Fraser points out, in a 2-year period this leaves the offender with 17,502 hours in which to commit further crimes. The service itself changed: 'No longer were they to concentrate on supervising low-risk first- and second-time offenders in a bid to divert them from a life of crime; their new mission was to divert persistent offenders from prison by persuading courts to place them on probation, in the mistaken belief that by so doing, they could reform them.'[25]

This both stemmed from and encouraged the virus which has overtaken the criminal justice system. Training manuals for the service are full of references to the 'processes of structural oppression, race, class and gender' and other such clichés of politically correct jargon.[26] So it was not surprising – even if it was bonkers – that in 1993 the National Association of Probation Officers' annual conference was moved from Bridlington because it was considered to be 'racist and heterosexual'.[27] And in the 'you couldn't make it up' category, in 1994 a local service paid substantial compensation and offered an apology to a drug dealer for his 'hurt feelings' after he read a probation report recommending a long prison sentence. The dealer read the report as he waited for sentencing and was caused to have a 'high anxiety level'.[28] In 2001, one local probation service spent £60,000 on 'gender awareness' training – compared with just £4000 on training to do with working with criminals.[29]

Worse still, the use of cautions has become akin to a reward for criminals. If they admit an offence, the police have the right to administer a caution and thus save the bother of a charge and a court hearing. They do so with astonishing frequency, and not just for minor offences: in 2000, cautions were handed out for violence (19,900), robbery (600), fraud (6200), drug offences (41,100), public order (13,400), burglary (6600), theft and handling stolen goods (67,600), criminal damage (3200), assault (15,500), car theft (4300) and a further 35,200 other summary offences.[30] Today, 300,000 offenders a year are let off with a caution. Although there is no reliable way of knowing how many offenders handed cautions reoffend, we do know – because they end up in court years later – that many thousands are given repeat cautions.

In a similar vein, in 2006 over 160,000 offenders caught causing 'disorder' (7 types of offence including shoplifting, criminal damage, being drunk and disorderly, and 'causing harassment, alarm or distress') were, under a new scheme introduced in 2002, handed £50 or £80 penalty notices – accounting for one in nine crimes solved by the police.

The attraction to the police of these methods for dealing with crime is that they count as successful detection, boosting Home Office clear-up targets, even though the penalties do not lead to a criminal record or even an admission of guilt by the offender. So it is no wonder that their use has exploded, from 58,706 penalty notices in 2004 for the 7 'disorder' offences to 137,333 in 2005, and 167,000 in 2006.[31]

The police claim in mitigation that they are severely under-resourced and have to act within manpower constraints. But the figures show that this is sophistry. In 1901 the population of England and Wales was 32,527,843 and there were 42,484 police – one for every 765 people. In 1951 the population was 43,745,000; there were 63,116 police – one for every 693 people. And in 2001 the population was 53,137,000, with 127,231 police – one for every 417 people. There are far more per head than ever before. What has changed, of course, is what those police actually do.

There are frequent calls from politicians and the public for the return of 'the bobby on the beat'. It is not just common sense that criminals will be less likely to commit a crime if they know that a policeman may, literally, be just round the corner. It is also statistically proven. In March 1982 two American researchers, George Kelling and James Q. Wilson, wrote a seminal article in the *Atlantic Monthly*, which showed how 'having officers walk beats did in fact make their neighborhoods safer'. That article gave rise to what has come to be known as the 'broken windows' theory, more of which later.

The 1962 Royal Commission on policing concluded

that it was important to have 'a sufficient quantity of constables on beat duty in close touch with the public'. And the then Commissioner of the Met, Sir Joseph Simpson, concurred: 'The policeman in a car, on a motorcycle or absent from his beat becomes a cypher.'[32] But within ten years the bobby on the beat was a dying breed. Why? Largely because of the influence of one man, Eric St Johnston, Chief Constable of Lancashire, Chief Inspector of Constabulary and adviser to politicians and the Home Office. Peter Hitchens writes in his *Brief History of Crime* that St Johnston 'saw himself as the first of a new generation of visionary police chiefs'.[33] One of the few graduates in the force, he was admired both by Roy Jenkins, the Home Secretary, and Harold Wilson, the Prime Minister (who later penned an admiring preface to St Johnston's autobiography).

The Lancashire force was one of the largest in the land, and had traditionally been innovative, introducing radio communication in 1936 and speed traps in 1957, for instance. But the most profound change was the introduction of panda cars (named after their bold colour scheme) to police the rough area of Kirkby in Liverpool. As St Johnston put it: 'We were unable to find enough policemen to send to Kirkby and we had at the most only six uniformed men patrolling the town at any one time, and this in a community which had risen to 60,000 by 1963.'[34] But, as Hitchens writes: 'It was the pivotal moment in the history of policing and crime prevention in modern Britain. While it offered a short-term answer to a special problem, it would come to affect the whole country in an astonishingly short time.' The use of panda cars rather than bobbies on the beat was cheaper; it seemed to be successful.

Soon the idea was copied everywhere: 'It was revolution by secret decree.'[35] And a remarkably stupid one at that, as it did not take long for criminals to realize that most of the country now had no regular police presence. It wasn't just the absence of foot patrols; many police stations, too, were closed down on the back of management consultant recommendations and supposed efficiency gains. In the words of the Audit Commission (in March 1999): it was necessary to rationalize 'the management of the police estate' because 'opportunities to generate income and reduce costs through rationalisation are being missed'. Rochester Row and other large central police stations across the country were sold as real estate; some were switched to part-time opening (as if criminals would restrict their activities to coincide with their opening hours!). Between 1990 and 2000, 650 stations were shut in England and Wales. By 2002, not only had a third of all stations shut; 60 per cent of those left open were only open during office hours.[36]

The fundamental problem is that the public and the elites who run the criminal justice system inhabit two different worlds. In one world – the real one – knife crime is a threat, muggings and robberies are on the rise and the police and criminal justice system appear to be more troubled by suspects' rights than their duty to protect the public; in the other world, the concerns are how to manage the system and how best to treat criminals for their social problems, since it is society's ills which create crime through poor housing, unemployment, bad schooling and poverty. This was taken to its logical extreme in the experience of one woman in 1999, as reported in the *Daily Mail*:

When Rebecca Trebble found that her car had been vandalised, she expected the police to treat her as a victim of a crime. Even when they told her they were not sending an officer to investigate what they regarded as a minor matter, she thought they would at least care about her plight. But when she wrote to them complaining about her treatment, the local police chief in Taunton, Somerset, replied that whoever had damaged her car was a victim deserving of sympathy too. Superintendent John Snell wrote back: 'Whilst I have every sympathy with you being the victim of crime, the position regarding victims is not limited to those who suffer as you have done. Many of those who are responsible for the commission of such minor crimes could be considered to be victims themselves. To my knowledge some of our prolific offenders are heroin addicts who live in the very worst housing conditions in our area in relative poverty. It is also true many of them are from broken homes and really have miserable family backgrounds. I know this is no excuse and it is difficult to sympathise with such individuals when they commit crime; however, I do think sometimes we should give a thought to those less fortunate than ourselves.' Miss Trebble, a 21-year-old financial assistant, said yesterday: 'I was shocked. I felt I was being patronised and that he was lecturing me. To suggest the criminal was as much the victim was amazing. That's just not what you expect from the police.'[37]

If this were not an entirely logical development from such victim theories, it would be shocking. No less shocking in its own way is the following anecdote, recalled by the writer Charles Murray:

> A fortnight before we [Murray and Una Padel, the director of the Centre for Crime and Justice Studies, a research foundation that advocates alternatives to prison and restorative justice] talked, her 13-year-old daughter had been mugged. If the muggers could be brought to account (they cannot, even though the daughter knows who they are), what would Padel have in mind for them? True to her principles, she does not want the muggers jailed. 'I remain angry with them, but I don't want anything horrible to happen to them,' she said. 'I want them to stop robbing people, that's the bottom line . . . In an ideal world I would like them to be made aware of the impact they've actually had on my daughter and, ideally, apologise.'[38]

Chilling in its liberalism.

And thus a phrase such as New Labour's 'tough on crime, tough on the causes of crime' can have a real meaning despite being literally meaningless. 'Tough on crime' sends a political signal to voters, despite an almost total lack of action in government; 'tough on the causes of crime' sends a political slogan to the left and to the establishment, despite there being, in reality, no 'causes' of crime beyond criminal actions.

Take drug crime. The received wisdom is that drug-related crime is proof of the victimhood of the offender, addicted to an illegal substance and barely responsible for his action, driven to crime by the need to satisfy his habit. He needs treatment, not punishment. But widespread though this notion is now, it is wrong. It is not drug addicts who turn to crime; it is criminals who turn to drugs. A study conducted by the NHS in 1998 and kept as quiet as possible because its findings were inconvenient[39] examined 1000 drug users. The study found that even when on methadone the offenders continued to commit crimes. In another study in 2000, 221 addicts treated in a London clinic were examined to assess the impact of methadone on their offending. The treatment was found to have no impact on their non-drug-related crime.[40] And a study in 1999 by South Bank University's criminal policy research unit found that most drug-using criminals were career criminals long before their drug use began.

But the notion that criminals are responsible for their own behaviour, rather than being the victims of circumstance and society, is directly contrary to the 'new criminology', as it is called. The root of this now dominant doctrine stems from the pernicious influence of Professor Leslie Wilkins. His study of wartime children concluded that they were 'exceptionally delinquent', which he argued stemmed from the stress of social and family conditions during the war years. This research formed the foundation of analyses which suggested that crime itself stemmed from the stresses caused by factors such as poverty, upbringing, unemployment and education. The real blame for crime – and thus the opportunity for its cure – lay not with the criminal, who was himself a victim, but society. Books such as Ian Taylor, Paul Walton and Jock Young's *The New*

Criminology: For a Social Theory of Deviance argued that:
'We are confronted once again with the central question of
man's relationship to structures of power, domination and
authority – and the ability of men to confront these
structures in acts of crime, deviance and dissent.'[41] The
rot began in 1959 with a Home Office publication, *Penal
Practice in a Changing Society*, which talked about the
'environmental' dimensions of crime, stressed the need
for more research into its 'varied and complex causes' and
abjectly failed to offer any evidence for such dimensions
and causes. The 1960s saw a flood of similar papers, posit-
ing factors such as the 'inner conflicts' of adolescence, the
environmental pressures of school, housing, gangs and
youth culture, 'rapid social change' and more or less any
other excuse one can think of.[42] Howard Jones's *Crime in
a Changing Society* talked of the need for the criminal justice
system to 'become an effective agency of treatment', and for
diagnosis of offenders' problems and sentencing to be transferred from courts to a new treatment body.[43]

Organizations such as the Howard League for Penal
Reform, the Prison Reform Trust and the National
Association for the Care and Resettlement of Offenders fed
and fed again off this wave of anti-prison, anti-punishment
dogma, often spouting utter nonsense as fact. In 1993, for
instance, NACRO claimed that 88 per cent of adult ex-
offenders and 80 per cent of young ex-offenders on their
training schemes did not reoffend, a statement which to
this day they have not substantiated with evidence, and
which flies against other known evidence on reoffending.[44]
It would, had it been true, have signalled a breakthrough in
human existence – a permanent solution to the problem of

crime. Not that it was just outsiders who pushed this line. The judiciary itself is infected from top to bottom with the same virus. The Lord Chief Justice ruled in 2002 that first-time non-violent domestic burglars should not be sent to prison; the 'starting point' of up to eighteen months in prison no longer applied and courts should impose a community sentence in the first instance.[45]

Influential – indeed, dominant – as such views became, they are ideologically driven, with no basis in fact. Take the view of prison which informs the idea that criminals need to be helped rather than punished. It is often argued that Britain is a violent society not because criminals are violent but because the state is violent – and that more people are jailed here than in other comparable EU countries. Britain certainly imprisons a higher percentage of its population. But this is a meaningless measure, since it takes no account of the extraordinary proportion of the UK population that commits crimes. Allowing for this, Britain has a *low* imprisonment rate. A scarcely credible 0.3 per cent of offences results in a prison sentence.[46] Indeed, British criminals are now living in a golden age. In 1954, one in three criminals convicted of robbery was sent down. In 1994, the proportion fell to one in twenty.

In the EU the average number of prisoners per 100,000 of the population in 2003 was 98, compared with 139 in England and Wales. But comparing the number of prisoners to the number of recorded crimes, the EU average was 17.5 and the figure for England and Wales was 12.4. Spain, for instance, imprisons 48 and Ireland 33. In fact, 8 out of 15 EU countries had rates of imprisonment for every 1000 crimes that were higher than England and Wales. If we imprisoned offenders at the EU average rate there would be 113,150 prisoners rather than 80,000. If we imprisoned at (socialist) Spain's rate, the England and Wales prison population would be about 369,000.[47]

If only. The statistic which has been proved in every instance across the globe but which is ignored by those who have shaped policy in recent decades is that high imprisonment rates correlate directly with low crime rates: Spain and Ireland, for example, both have far lower crime rates than Britain. And when Britain began increasing its prison population thirteen years ago, the number of crimes began falling. In 1993 the prison population was 49,000 and the number of recorded offences 19 million. By 2005 the prison population was 75,000 and the number of crimes 11 million. The same story can be told for the US, and indeed everywhere where imprisonment rates are high: the crime rate has fallen steadily as the prison population has climbed. A Civitas study shows how clear the link is:

> For crimes such as robbery, burglary, car theft and assault, increasing the risk of imprisonment has produced a fall in crime in the USA. It appears to be less effective for murder and rape and we may conjecture that this is because the motives or emotional drives leading to these offences are less subject to rational calculation. Where the crimes are calculated to acquire material possessions, potential offenders may be more likely to weigh up the risk of being punished. People addicted to drugs are an exception – but it is a truism to say that they are not likely to be thinking clearly, precisely because they have fallen

under the sway of a narcotic substance . . . Two effects led to the fall in crime in America. First, there was a deterrent effect and second, an incapacitation effect . . . A criminal cannot commit offences in the wider society while he is in prison, but a person under a community sentence can . . . Prison works as a method of protecting the public and deterring criminals, but some commentators are reluctant to accept the truth of this conclusion because they feel that punishment and the rehabilitation of offenders are mutually exclusive alternatives. Prison is certainly a punishment, but it is not *only* a punishment. It is also a means of protecting the public from known offenders and of deterring others. It is also – as the Prison Service fully acknowledges – an opportunity to reform criminals in the hope of encouraging a law-abiding lifestyle on release. And, as the Prison Service freely admits, efforts to reform prisoners are much in need of improvement. Measures intended to rehabilitate offenders while they are in custody need to be quickly and substantially stepped up. Much has been learnt about how to discourage anti-social attitudes, to create a stronger moral sense, and to encourage a more positive attitude in convicted criminals. But while their offending continues, it is preferable to rehabilitate them in prison, so that members of the public continue to be protected.[48]

None of this is mere assertion; it is all demonstrable, not least the point that when they are incarcerated, criminals cannot offend – a statement of the obvious which is all but universally ignored by the criminal justice system. The American Bureau of Justice Statistics showed that the increase in the US prison population between 1975 and 1989 reduced violent crime by 10–15 per cent, preventing a minimum of 390,000 murders, rapes, robberies and assaults.[49]

In 1997 (when Labour took office) there were about 61,000 criminals in jail. The July 2008 figure was 83,575. One needs to ask a simple question: how many crimes would have been committed if those additional 22,000 offenders had not been imprisoned? David Green of Civitas offers an answer:

> The best evidence comes from a Home Office survey in 2000. Offenders about to start a prison sentence were asked how many crimes they had committed in the previous 12 months. The average was 140 crimes a year and, for those on drugs, 257. The Government has been trying to limit prison to the most serious offenders and we know that the majority of prison inmates have a drug or alcohol problem. The average today is, therefore, likely to be nearer 257 crimes than 140.
>
> If we take the lower figure, incapacitating 22,000 criminals who would have committed 140 crimes a year prevents more than three million crimes. If they were all drug users the figure would exceed five million. Could the increase in the prison population from 2006–07 to 2007–08 explain the fall in crime over the same period? Police-recorded crime fell by 476,900 offences. Between April 2007 and April 2008 the prison population increased by 1,843. If the annual offending rate was 140, then 258,000 crimes would have been prevented. If the additional prisoners were all serious offenders, as

the Government claims, then 473,000 crimes would
have been prevented.[50]

The contrast is clear. One only needs to turn the clock
back a few years to the time as Home Secretary of one of
the most craven, complacent, conceited and catastrophic
public figures of recent years: Douglas Hurd. Lord Hurd
could be attacked equally soundly for his time as Foreign
Secretary in standing by and watching Slobodan Milošević's
ethnic cleansing, in capitulating on every issue of consequence to do with the EU, and in upholding all the worst
aspects of Foreign Office tradition. But it was as Home
Secretary that he did most damage to the British people,
presiding over record crime increases, allowing more
criminals to roam the streets than any previous Home
Secretary and ruling out any notion of reducing crime.
Hurd's philosophy was the Home Office's at its worst: that
the purpose of policy was to stem the increase in crime.
The idea of reducing it was laughed out of court. No
liberal penal policy idea was too much for Hurd; any idea
of punishment was too much to contemplate. When he
was Home Secretary, from 1985 to October 1989, Lord
Hurd set out to reduce the prison population. The consequence was a rapid increase in crime. As David Green writes:
'There were 46,800 prisoners in 1985 rising to 50,000 in
1988 as judges responded to the crime wave. Instead of
backing the judges, Lord Hurd cut the prison population
so that it fell to 45,600 soon after he left. Crime under the
British Crime Survey rose from 12.4 million offences in
1985 to more than 14 million in 1989, and police records
show an increase from 3.6 million in 1985 to 4.5 million in

1990.'[51] If he had any sense of propriety, Hurd would have crawled into a cave many years ago in recognition of his dreadful record in all areas of ministerial life. And yet even today he still bangs the drum for reducing prison numbers as chairman of the Prison Reform Trust.

Equally ignored by the criminal justice system is the success of the 'broken windows' theory. As its authors, Kelling and Wilson, put it: 'Consider a building with a few broken windows. If the windows are not repaired, the tendency is for vandals to break a few more windows. Eventually, they may even break into the building, and if it's unoccupied, perhaps become squatters or light fires inside. Or consider a sidewalk. Some litter accumulates. Soon, more litter accumulates. Eventually, people even start leaving bags of trash from take-out restaurants there or breaking into cars.'[52] Instead of tolerating 'minor' crime to focus on major crimes, the police target all criminals. This is sometimes known as 'zero tolerance', but the term is somewhat misleading. The real point is that there is no such thing as minor crime in isolation. Not only does it spread; it also leads to other, bigger crimes.

This is the real story behind the much (and rightly) heralded turnaround in New York City. In 1998, the Home Secretary Jack Straw was reported as being 'in shock' after reading a report by Professors David Farrington and Patrick Langan, two of the country's leading criminologists, which showed that crime was, in most areas, worse in the UK than the US. There had, for instance, been an 81 per cent increase in robbery since 1981 here; in the US there had been a 28 per cent fall. The rate of muggings was 1.4 times higher in the UK than the US.[53] The trend has continued:

between 1991 and 2007, robberies more than doubled in London (from 22,000 to 46,000). In New York, they fell to less than a quarter of the previous rate (99,000 to 24,000).

And guess what? In the one UK city in which a similar policy was attempted, the results were just as impressive. In Hartlepool in the mid-1990s, the then Detective Inspector Ray Mallon went out on a limb, defying his senior officers by following the 'broken windows' theory. Crime fell by over a third, and he was rewarded for his efforts by being suspended for four and a half years on misconduct charges. The public then made their feelings plain. In 2002 he was elected, running independently, as Mayor of Middlesbrough and was re-elected in 2007.

The priorities of criminal justice policy are now warped. Successive governments have talked tough on crime but acted soft. Even when they are caught, criminals convicted of many of the worst offences often now face nothing tougher than probation, fines or community service. Yet some crimes are pursued by the police with relentless action. Motorists are now targeted mercilessly by an army of cameras. In 1951 there were 536,000 cases of summary action (ranging from written warnings to court proceedings) for motoring offences. By 1991 the figure had risen to 8.3 million cases, and by 2004 to 13.5 million. This is only in small measure due to there being more cars: since 1951 the number of licensed vehicles has risen seven times, and the number of legal actions twenty-five times.

Contrast the treatment of motorists with the treatment of young offenders. The 1982 Criminal Justice Act was designed to make it very difficult for judges (even if they were so minded) to punish young criminals. Instead, they should be treated and counselled. The consequence, as David Fraser puts it, is that 'those muggers (the majority of whom are young offenders) who were among the tiny minority to be caught had even less chance of going to prison and therefore even less reason not to rob victims in the street. It should be no surprise, therefore, that the Home Office figures for 2000 reported that the numbers of offences committed by males under the age of eighteen years increased to 80,600.'[54] And still they do not learn. In June 2008, plans were announced to keep even more young criminals out of prison:

A shakeup of the youth justice system is being planned by ministers that would see a failing punitive policy replaced by a more welfare-oriented, early-intervention approach to dealing with children in trouble. As part of a youth crime action plan to be published this summer, the Home Office has recommended that responsibility and funding for tackling youth crime – including local youth offending teams – should be moved to new, local authority-run 'children's trusts' . . . An unpublished analysis by the children's and justice ministries shows that teenage reoffending rates have remained largely unchanged since 1997, and that the 'progressional' aspect of the system means that more and more teenagers are being locked up for breaches of punishments handed out for lesser offences. This has led ministers to believe that the number of children in the criminal justice system will only be reduced if the police are persuaded to concentrate on serious offending by teenagers, and to caution more and charge fewer teenagers in the case of minor offences.[55]

That one report encapsulates almost everything wrong with Britain's approach to crime: actively seeking to increase the proportion of crimes dealt with by cautions; reducing still further the numbers of criminals sent to prison; and a blinkered refusal to realize that it is the liberal establishment's proposed solutions to crime which make the situation worse.

8

FOOTBALL

20 May 1992

Open any newspaper and sport – to be precise, sports stars – will fill not just the back pages but much of the front, too. Their sporting antics are still at the back. But the stars themselves are now such über-celebrities that their movements are chronicled in the front half alongside – indeed more often than not ahead of – film and TV stars. They write (or have written for them) books which sell in the hundreds of thousands. David Beckham has, for instance, already published three volumes of autobiography: *Beckham: My World* in 2001, *David Beckham: My Side* in 2002, and *Beckham: Both Feet on the Ground* in 2003, with combined sales in the millions. The last of the three books sold 86,000 in its first two days on sale – 21,000 more than the combined shortlist for that year's Booker Prize managed in the whole year.

They pose for fashion shoots (for which David Beckham is now almost equally famous). They act in cameo film roles. Their sex lives are speculated over endlessly. So deeply entrenched in the national fabric have sports stars become that it is difficult to remember what a recent phenomenon this is. Barely more than a decade ago, sportsmen and women were, in the main, viewed as sweaty and dull. There were some sporting heroes who escaped from the back pages into the national consciousness, such as Sir Bobby Moore or Lester Piggott, and a few whose celebrity was a precursor to the modern phenomenon, such as George Best, but they were few and far between.

This changed on one day: Wednesday 20 May 1992, when Rupert Murdoch's BSkyB (Sky, as it is more colloquially known) paid £304 million for the exclusive rights to televise the newly formed football Premier League. From that day onwards, everything was different. Not only did sport enter a new world of celebrity, but the notion of celebrity itself changed for ever. And, on top of all of that, the top tier of English football became the greatest football league in the world – far and away so. This chapter explains how that happened and why it matters.

Rupert Murdoch first entered British public life in 1969, when he beat a £34 million offer from Robert Maxwell's Pergamon Press to become the new managing director of the *News of the World* newspaper. His acuity and shrewd positioning was a portend of his later manoeuvrings. Soon afterwards he bought a failing broadsheet, the *Sun*, and transformed it into Britain's biggest-selling daily newspaper by turning it tabloid, introducing the daily topless model on Page 3 and popularizing its news content. In 1981, he took over the sclerotic, loss-making *Times* and its sister paper, the hugely profitable *Sunday Times*. Taking on the malign and corrupt influence of the print unions, he endured a long-lasting and often violent dispute before achieving a complete victory, which transformed not only his own papers' prospects but also those of the entire market.

The British regulators frustrated Murdoch's initial attempts to establish a major presence in TV (although he had earlier rescued the nascent London Weekend Television), and it was only when the new technology of satellite TV emerged that he spotted a way in, foreseeing the possibility of huge profits. In 1983, News International set up the Sky Channel, a European satellite-to-cable broadcaster. The content – English-language sports and low-grade entertainment – was designed for the cable television systems which dominated the continental marketplace. But it was not a great success, bringing in only a few million pounds' annual advertising revenue. Murdoch was convinced, however, that the new direct satellite broadcasting technology could be far more lucrative, especially if aimed at the British market. Instead of having to pay cable providers for the rights to transmit the Sky Channel to their subscribers, direct satellite transmission offered a new model: broadcasters could provide multichannel programming directly to subscribers' homes through a satellite dish and decoder.

Satellite broadcasting also had the great advantage of being outside the existing broadcasting law, which limited terrestrial television to four channels: BBC1, BBC2, ITV and Channel 4. Cable TV was insignificant in the UK because the cable network itself was then insignificant – the full network was laid only in the mid-1990s. But when new rules were introduced for satellite broadcasting, putting a 20 per cent threshold on foreign ownership, the regulators ruled that Sky was ineligible for a licence because Sky's owner, the News International Corporation, was foreign-owned. So the exclusive British licence was given to a consortium of established British companies, joined under the banner of British Satellite Television. To most observers this looked like another knock-out blow to Murdoch's TV hopes. In hindsight, however, it was no more than a hiccup. Just as he had regularly outmanoeuvred and outsmarted the competition and regulators in his newspaper dealings, so too would he with satellite TV.

BSB (the name given to British Satellite Television's broadcast operation) was due to begin broadcasting in 1989. But it made the fatally misconceived decision to operate via its own newly built satellites, called Marco Polo 1 and 2, and using newly developed technology, D-MAC, to transmit to a new Philips-designed dish which it labelled the 'squarial'. Almost nothing worked. The launch was delayed for almost a year, until April 1990, and when it was finally up and running the few would-be customers found it almost impossible to find a squarial to buy. Worse, by the time of its delayed launch, BSB had a competitor: Sky TV. Murdoch had originally reacted to being refused a licence by attempting to join the BSB consortium but had got nowhere. So he decided to beat them at their own game. He began by renting space on the Luxembourg-based Astra satellites, thus falling outside the control of British broadcasting licensing laws. And rather than reinventing the perfectly serviceable existing PAL technology, he broadcast through it. Sky TV began transmission in 1989 with a souped-up version of the old Sky Channel, called Sky One; to that were added Eurosport, Sky Movies (which showed films for a fee) and a 24-hour news channel, Sky News.

By the time BSB had started to broadcast, Sky TV already had 750,000 satellite dishes up and running. Six months later, sales showed that there were nearly 1 million Sky TV dishes in use, compared to less than 120,000 BSB squarials. Just as VHS beat Betamax before the latter had a proper chance to compete, so BSB was blown out of the water before it ever really started. By November 1990, BSB had spent £800 million with no apparent possibility of ever recouping it – simply continuing in existence was costing the consortium another £8 million every week. But even if Sky looked the likely winner, such was the financial chaos that victory seemed certain to be Pyrrhic: the start-up cost was £122 million and the first-year losses were £95 million. While it lasted, the battle between BSB and Sky TV was fierce and astronomically loss-making for both. The then CNN owner, Ted Turner, rightly described the two companies as 'haemorrhaging red ink'. The over-whelming majority of observers thought that even if Sky TV was beating BSB into the ground, Murdoch was over-reaching himself financially and had finally bitten off more than he could chew. Indeed, the notion that his Sky losses could bring about the collapse of the whole Murdoch empire was widespread. The wiseacres concluded that Murdoch's growing struggle to meet the interest payments on News International's debts of more than £4.5 billion was a bridge too far for him.

But Murdoch has always had the last laugh. In July 1990, he met the head of the BSB consortium, Peter Davis, for dinner. Davis offered to buy Sky, in effect offering Murdoch a rescue plan to save News International from possible collapse. But for all the risk to his company, Murdoch was not interested in selling – not least because Sky looked to be in a far more promising position than BSB. Murdoch did not have the financial capacity of the BSB consortium's heavyweight members, and could not make a counter-offer to buy BSB. So a third option emerged: merger. To the astonishment of most observers, in November 1990 BSkyB was born, ownership divided 50–50 between Murdoch and the four BSB investors. The regulators immediately announced their opposition. There was, however, nothing they could do, since the new broadcaster would transmit, like Sky, through the Astra satellites. And the much-lampooned squarial would be discarded. But with combined losses of £10 million a week, most of the comment on the merger was based on the premise that this was the last, dying breath of an absurdly risky and expensive venture. Indeed, BSkyB's first week of operation saw a recorded loss of £14 million.

Whatever the financial arrangements, the merger soon came to seem more of a Sky takeover. The staff of the old Sky TV dominated the workforce, replacing almost all of the former BSB employees. But by far the most important appointment to the channel was a newcomer, New Zealander Sam Chisholm, as the new CEO. He came with a phenomenal track record. By thirty-five he had been appointed CEO of the Australian Channel 9 and over the next fifteen years he had turned it into Australia's largest

and most profitable TV station. Chisholm's impact at
BSkyB was immediate. In February 1991, the company
had come within minutes of being put into receivership
before 146 banks agreed to a £4.2 billion refinancing package. First, Chisholm reduced the number of staff from 4500
to 1000 and, with other measures, reduced the losses to
£1.6 million per week. But his real impact was on programming. Chisholm saw what many others did not fully
grasp: that the rights to broadcast live football were, as was
once said about traditional commercial TV, a licence to
print money.

The first regular TV sport began in 1954 when the BBC
launched *Sportsview*. Practical developments, such as the
start of floodlit football, made it possible to televise evening
and dark winter games. With the majority of the population having a TV by the 1960s, sport was helping to
promote TV and TV was helping to promote sport. In
1970, the World Cup in Mexico was screened live in
colour for the first time. But until the 1980s, almost all
sport was on the BBC. The rise of ITV had led the BBC
to tie organizers into long-term contracts which precluded
bidding wars. But even if the potential importance of football to TV was yet to be made as clear as it would later
become, the importance of TV to football was already
growing. In 1986, the Football League received £6.3 million for a 2-year broadcasting rights agreement.

In 1988, there was a strong rumour that BSB was
making a lavish bid for the rights to broadcast the First
Division. Greg Dyke, then the Chief Executive of London
Weekend Television and, crucially, chairman of the ITV

Association and ITV Sport, decided that 'my job was to derail the process and pinch these live football rights from BSB'.[1] In alliance with David Dein, the Deputy Chairman of Arsenal and one of the key movers and shakers at the Football League, he concocted a plan: 'We would go direct to the big five clubs of the day – Arsenal, Liverpool, Manchester United, Tottenham and Everton – and offer them a minimum of £1 million a year each for the exclusive rights to broadcast their home matches. This was massively more than any of them had received in the past. The Football League could sell the rest of the old First Division matches to whomever they wanted, but of course without the big clubs' home games they were worth much less.'[2] Dyke was convinced that he had the support of the big five clubs and extended the secret offer to five others. The league panicked, fearing a breakaway by the ten clubs, and opened formal negotiations with ITV, effectively ditching BSB. A deal was done: £11 million a year for 21 live games, to be played mostly on Sunday afternoons. The announcement killed off – temporarily – a national institution. Because ITV had won the rights, the Saturday-evening BBC staple of *Match of the Day* was off the screens, a change to traditional viewing habits which sent some people apoplectic.

The reverberations were enormous. First, the negotiations had opened the eyes of the bigger clubs to the possibilities which direct control of their own broadcasting rights might bring, laying the seed of the formation of the Premiership. But in a mind-numbingly stupid and counterproductive move, the lesser clubs of the Second Division were so annoyed at being outmanoeuvred by the bigger

First Division clubs that they joined together and took control of the league, ousting Dein from the management committee and forcing the removal of the chairman of Everton from the chairmanship of the league. From that moment on, the creation of the Premiership became a certainty; there was no way the big clubs would allow their financial potential to be stifled by the petty-minded jealousy of the small clubs. By 17 July 1991, a Founder Members' Agreement had been established with the basic principles for setting up what became the FA Premier League. Critically, it would negotiate its own broadcast and sponsorship agreements. At the end of the 1991–2 season, the First Division clubs resigned en masse from the Football League and, on 27 May, together formed the FA Premier League.

But when it came to negotiating the rights to televise the Premier League, ITV was no longer merely negotiating with the clubs and outwitting the BBC and the less than brilliant BSB team; it was also up against Rupert Murdoch. (Although, initially, Sam Chisholm had tried to team up with ITV. According to Greg Dyke: 'He was pretty blunt. He told me that Rupert Murdoch had approved what he was about to say. "Mr Dyke," he said, "why don't we get together to fuck these football clubs?" My view was that if he wanted a deal with us it meant we were in prime position and didn't need him. How wrong I was.'[3]) The dynamic had changed, too. Tottenham Hotspur had been sold to Alan Sugar, whose company was the main supplier of satellite dishes to Sky. Dyke appears not to have realized quite how determined Murdoch was to secure the rights and was convinced that the ITV bid was high enough; but on the morning of the crucial vote by the teams, Sugar was heard speaking on the phone: 'You've got to blow them out of the water.'[4] The reasonable assumption is that he was talking to Murdoch or Chisholm. As a club chairman, Sugar had heard that the initial Sky–BBC bid (Sky's agreement with the BBC was for the corporation to show recorded highlights on the revived *Match of the Day*) fell short of ITV's offer of £262 million. It is said that Chisholm rang Murdoch to persuade him that he had to break the bank to win. A new Sky bid arrived: £304 million.

But it was more than money that won the vote for Sky. Murdoch himself took charge of the personal aspects of the bid, wooing and flattering the key decision-makers. Rick Parry, who had been recruited from Ernst & Young to set up the Premier League (and later became its chief executive), was flown to the Sky call centre in Scotland to see just how impressive the operation was. He later described Murdoch as 'the most impressive man I ever met'.[5]

With football the big lure, Chisholm was able to position Sky as a premium-content, subscription-backed channel – a strategy that quickly proved successful. In its first 30 days offering football, Sky sold over 100,000 digiboxes. When the crafty decision was taken to offer them for free, and remove one of the main drags on new subscribers, it took just ten months to add 1.2 million to the roster. By the end of Sky's 1993 fiscal year, it was making an operating profit of nearly £186 million. By 1996 its revenues were over £1 billion, with pre-tax profits of £257 million. Sky's success was built primarily on football; the 1992 deal was cheap at the price. It subsequently paid

£670 million in 1997, £1.2 billion in 2001, £1.024 billion in 2004 and, for the 2007–10 rights (shared with Setanta due to EU rules), £1.2 billion.

The money that has flooded into football has changed not merely the game – the influx of foreign players has been revolutionary – but the way the game is perceived. Before Sky's money poured in, players in the old First Division were lucky to be paid £80,000 a year; today, many will leave their club in anger if they are not given a salary of £80,000 a week. Players' negotiations with the clubs are treated as front-page news. When Manchester United's Portuguese winger, Cristiano Ronaldo, was being wooed by Real Madrid in the summer of 2008, the 'will he, won't he?' saga was played out in the main news sections; his performance at Euro 2008 was kept to the back pages.

Nothing exemplified this change more than the growth of the global brand of Posh and Becks. Such is the international superstar status of David Beckham that it is easy to forget that he was once known only as a footballer, albeit one on whom the nation sometimes came to depend as England captain. But as soon as he started to date Victoria Adams – Posh Spice from the Spice Girls pop band – he moved from the back to the front pages. The couple – from then on universally known as Posh and Becks – became the most famous husband and wife on the planet and the perfect example of the sum of two parts being far, far greater than their individual properties. When Beckham was sold in July 2003 by Manchester United to Real Madrid for £24.5 million, it was something of a bargain. On one level he might have been bought for his footballing skill; but the real purpose of the move was to utilize the Beckham brand. The Spanish club sold a million Beckham shirts within six months of his arrival. According to Real's marketing director, José Sánchez: 'In the four years that Beckham played in Madrid we generated more than £300 million in commercial activities. In the time that Beckham was here, profits from merchandising increased by 137 per cent.'[6] As if to show that Beckham was, above all, a global brand, in January 2007 the footballer signed a contract with Los Angeles Galaxy – a five-year deal worth £128 million. *France Football* magazine calculated that his earnings from salary and endorsements rose to €31 million (£24.7 million) in the year after his move. Beckham's arrival in LA was part of a strategy by the US Major League Soccer to replicate the success of the Premiership (as the Premier League had become known). The Premiership is now behind only the NFL, Major League Baseball and the NBA in terms of financial success. In terms of its global reach and popularity, it leaves those US competitors far behind. Part of that success is down to the origins of its players, which are equally global in scope. Players from 89 countries have participated in the league and in 2007/8, 64 nationalities were represented among its 20 clubs. And it is a British triumph: conceived and executed in Britain, for Britain and the world.

It was not just footballers who became celebrities – it was their Wives and Girlfriends, too. Pictures of footballers in nightclubs with their women draped over their arms soon became pictures of the women without the footballers, often in specially posed modelling spreads. The WAG nonpareil was Coleen McLoughlin. She had nothing to commend her to the public other than her relationship with Wayne Rooney, the (then) Evertonian wunderkind. She could not sing. She could not act. She was plain to look at. She had, in effect, no marketable skills. But none of that mattered. By 2008 she was regarded as one of the style icons of the country, a staple of the newspapers, pictured nipping in and out of boutiques and restaurants. Both she and Wayne Rooney released autobiographies in 2007. Coleen's *Welcome to My World* easily outsold Wayne's *My Story So Far*. By the age of 20 she was said to have a fortune of £5.5 million, thanks to endorsement deals with Diet Coke, LG Chocolate phones and Asda's 'George' line of cheap clothing.[7] Her fame was nationwide, thanks to nothing other than being with a footballer. Coleen and Wayne's wedding took place in June 2008 on the Italian Riviera and was covered, appropriately enough, exclusively in *Hello!* – the fee was said to be £1.5 million.

So successful is the Premiership, with its clubs now able to lure the greatest players and the wealthiest patrons on the planet, that it is easy to forget how bad things were for football in the 1970s and 1980s. As a decade, the 1970s are now a byword for the drab and dour. And football was no different. English football had lost much of the glamour that came from winning the 1966 World Cup and was instead insular, violent and depressing. The problem of hooliganism, which dogged English football for years, was not merely attached to football; in many ways, it was *caused* by football.

Don Revie is now an almost forgotten figure, remembered only for the sudden manner of his leaving his job as England manager to earn a fast buck in the Middle East.

But he was, in his time, a key influence not just on football and sport generally but on society itself; his behaviour was emblematic of society as a whole. Revie took a team on the brink of Third Division obscurity, Leeds United, and turned it into one of the most powerful and feared teams in Europe. In an era when English football could boast some of its most famous and charismatic managers – Nicholson, Busby, Shankly, Clough, Allison, Mercer, Ramsey – Revie and his team stood out from the rest. They stood out because the manner in which he brought success represented a new and wholly malign development within football, which had serious consequences both inside and outside the game. Revie's achievements were built on his players' violent conduct, his own shady dealings – he tried (unsuccessfully) to bribe the opposing Bury team before a relegation struggle – and a fan following which was effectively encouraged to be as violent as their team. Leeds played dirty as a deliberate tactic to win at all costs, hacking opponents and intimidating referees. The leading referee of the time, Clive Thomas, said that with its relentless harassment and contesting of decisions on the field, Don Revie's Leeds United gave him more trouble than all other First Division clubs put together. Other teams were forced to respond in order to compete, spreading the cancer throughout the game. Indeed, when Revie left Leeds it collapsed – the club was relegated to the Second Division just seven years after they had reached the European Cup final.

The lesson was obvious – playing the Revie way worked. But it was a terrible lesson which brought football almost to the point of collapse in the 1970s and much of the 1980s, during which time the culture of violence moved from the pitch to the terraces and out into the streets. Revie represents – and was in part responsible for – everything bad about British sport and sporting attitudes in those benighted decades. Many 1980s stadiums were decrepit and there was little drive to do anything about it – not least because club owners thought that if they improved facilities they would soon be vandalized. And then, following the death in 1985 of 39 fans at Heysel Stadium in Belgium ahead of Liverpool's European Cup final against Juventus, English teams were banned from European competition. As if that were not bad enough, in 1989 96 fans died and over 150 were injured in a crush at Hillsborough during the FA Cup semi-final between Liverpool and Nottingham Forest. The government asked Lord Justice Taylor to look into the incident and make recommendations; the most important was for all-seater stadiums. The sheer cost of implementing the recommendations was one of the main prompts behind the idea of a breakaway league, to maximize TV revenue to fund the stadium improvements. But even the most optimistic club chairman never believed that the success of a breakaway league would be quite so stunning.

And yet, in typically British fashion, the Premier League is a regular source of moaning. It is too predictable. It is too expensive. It is full of foreigners. It is . . . blah, blah, blah. The purchase in 2008 of Manchester City by Arab billionaires prompted another round of the usual carping. And yet look at what the influx of such vast fortunes has meant: as a Spurs fan, I loathe the idea of Chelsea winning anything. But as a football fan, I can only celebrate that it is English teams which billionaires such as Roman Abramovich want to buy, and it is English teams which can now afford to buy the best players on the planet, for my enjoyment when I watch them play. By transforming British football from the deathly collapse of the 1980s into a magnet for success, the Premier League has meant football fans are now able to watch sport of a different calibre altogether from that offered just two decades ago. And that is a wonderful triumph, which can be dated to that one day in May 1992 when Sky bought the rights to Premiership football.

9

JIHADIST ISLAM

14 February 1989

On 14 February 1989, a fatwa requiring the execution of Salman Rushdie was proclaimed on Radio Tehran by Ayatollah Khomeini, the Supreme Leader of the Islamic Republic of Iran. *The Satanic Verses*, declared Khomeini, was 'blasphemous against Islam'. To secure Rushdie's death was a religious duty placed upon all Muslims. And that duty included inducing non-Muslims to carry out the act. To that end, a bounty was offered.

Khomeini's fatwas were no theological posits: they were real harbingers of death. He issued his first in 1947, against an Iranian government minister; the minister was shot dead. Many others later died on Khomeini's direct orders.

The fatwa against Rushdie read, in full:

In the name of God the Almighty. We belong to God and to Him we shall return. I would like to inform all intrepid Muslims in the world that the author of the book *Satanic Verses*, which has been compiled, printed, and published in opposition to Islam, the Prophet, and the Koran, and those publishers who were aware of its contents, are sentenced to death. I call on all zealous Muslims to execute them quickly, where they find them, so that no one will dare to insult the Islamic sanctities. Whoever is killed on this path will be regarded as a martyr, God willing. In addition, if anyone has access to the author of the book but does not possess the power to execute him, he should point him out to the people so that he may be punished for his actions. May God's blessing be on you all.

Ruhollah Musavi al-Khomeini.

Sir Ahmed Salman Rushdie was born in 1947 in Mumbai, the son of a lawyer-cum-businessman and a teacher. After a spell at the Cathedral and John Connon School in Mumbai (which describes itself as 'undoubtedly one of the most prestigious educational institutions in India') he was sent to Rugby School in England. He read history at King's College, Cambridge, and then spent a short time in advertising before becoming a full-time writer. His first book passed virtually unnoticed but his second, *Midnight's Children*, an allegory of the story of India during the move to independence, won the Booker Prize in 1981 and has subsequently won two 'Booker of Bookers' prizes, in 1993 and 2008. But, successful as *Midnight's Children* was, it was only with his fourth novel, *The Satanic Verses*, that Rushdie's name entered mass public consciousness (an understatement: his name became one of the best-known on the planet).

The reaction to *The Satanic Verses* was immediate on its publication on 26 September 1988. The title refers to a highly contentious Muslim legend in which Mohammed was tricked by the devil into adding false satanic verses to the Koran. In Rushdie's version, the Prophet Mahound is the founder of a religion called Submission, and lies to the people of Jahilia to gain power. Such mockery of Mohammed and Islam was a red rag to a bull and within days of its publication there were protests and ceremonial book-burnings in many Muslim areas. The book was said – entirely wrongly – to have portrayed Mohammed as a brothel keeper and to have called Muslims sons of whores. And it was attacked for not being 'accurate' in its depiction of Islam, as if fiction had to conform to the dictates of mullahs when referring to the religion.

The book was banned across the world, first in India nine days after publication and then in Bangladesh, Indonesia, Kenya, Singapore, Sudan, South Africa, Sri Lanka, Tanzania, Thailand and Venezuela. Bookshops were bombed and set ablaze by mobs. Ten thousand Muslims tried to storm the British High Commission in Delhi. The Japanese translator was stabbed to death in Tokyo. Six people were killed by police gunfire in America during a riot against the book. Thirty-seven people died in Turkey and the book's Norwegian publisher was shot three times and left for dead.

Within the UK there were mass Muslim protests in which the book was ceremonially burned. In April 1989, two London shops (Collets and Dillons) were bombed on one day. Liberty was bombed because it had a Penguin bookshop (Penguin published the book) inside. Bombs were found in bookshops across the country. And in August, Mustafa Mahmoud Mazeh died in his Paddington hotel room as the bomb intended for Rushdie blew up.

Many of the UK's most prominent Muslims were open and explicit in their support for the fatwa and their demand that the book be withdrawn from sale. Iqbal Sacranie remarked of the fatwa that: 'Death, perhaps, is a bit too easy for him . . . his mind must be tormented for the rest of his life unless he asks for forgiveness to Almighty Allah.'[1] (Today, Sacranie no longer calls for Rushdie's death and has been knighted for his services to the Muslim community.) Other mainstream Muslims joined in the book burnings.

Not that the reaction against the book was entirely spontaneous. Much of the ferment in Britain – and elsewhere – was the result of protests engineered by various radical Islamic groups, organizations funded by Saudi and Iranian money. The Saudis and the Iranians were engaged in the first stages of a battle for supremacy as the leading global Islamic power – a battle which remains pivotal today. After the initial success in India, the Islamic Foundation of Leicester (funded by Saudi Arabia) began agitating in Britain, a cause then given proper organization by Jamaat-i-Islami, the Pakistani Islamist party (see below). The Saudis also financed the United Kingdom Action Committee on Islamic Affairs, the group set up to coordinate the attacks on the book.

Rushdie was forced to live under police protection for nine years and has said that he moved house every three days. Four days after the fatwa, he tried to diffuse the maelstrom around him with an apology. The Iranian President,

Ali Khamenei, had appeared to indicate in a statement that if Rushdie 'apologizes and disowns the book, people may forgive him'. Rushdie responded the next day by saying how he regretted 'profoundly the distress the publication has occasioned to the sincere followers of Islam. Living as we do in a world of many faiths, this experience has served to remind us that we must all be conscious of the sensibilities of others.'[2] His words made no difference. Ayatollah Khomeini's office issued a statement:

The imperialist foreign media falsely alleged that the officials of the Islamic Republic have said the sentence of death on the author of *The Satanic Verses* will be retracted if he repents. Imam Khomeini has said: 'This is denied 100 per cent. Even if Salman Rushdie repents and becomes the most pious man of all time, it is incumbent on every Muslim to employ everything he has got, his life and wealth, to send him to Hell. If a non-Muslim becomes aware of Rushdie's whereabouts and has the ability to execute him quicker than Muslims, it is incumbent on Muslims to pay a reward or a fee in return for this action.'[3]

The statement could hardly be described as leaving room for negotiation; and nor could the break in diplomatic relations with Britain which the Iranians announced on 7 March 1989.

Rushdie is now able to live something close to a normal life and has developed a reputation as something of a man about town, not least for his liaisons with women. But the fatwa has never, contrary to many people's assumption, been lifted. Negotiations to restore diplomatic relations between Iran and the UK led to a deal in 1998 by which the then Iranian leader, Muhammad Khatami, said that the Iranian government would 'neither support nor hinder assassination operations on Rushdie'.[4] And that has somehow been taken as sufficient a climb-down by the Iranians for the UK government to resume relations – even though, in 2005, the Iranian spiritual leader and former president Ayatollah Ali Khamenei made it clear that the position remains exactly the same and the fatwa is extant.

Rushdie was awarded a knighthood for services to literature in June 2007. It would be wrong not to acknowledge that it was, on one level, an important signal that the British state would not be cowed. It led, inevitably, to mass protests by Muslim nations, with large demonstrations in Pakistan and Malaysia.

For Rushdie, the implications of the fatwa were immediately obvious and frightening. Less obvious but in hindsight even more serious was the implication for the future of what one might call British values. Britain was once renowned for its resolve against tyranny and its willingness to stand up to threats against our liberties. Our fight against the Third Reich appeared doomed to many but still we fought. We took on the IRA and won, forcing its leaders to concede that the armed struggle could not succeed and to sue for peace.

Today, we face an unprecedented terror assault from militant Islam. Instead of resisting, however, most of the British establishment has caved in. It was not, for instance, Britain which severed relations with Iran in protest after its government demanded the murder of a British citizen. It was Iran which broke off relations with Britain because, as the Iranian government put it at the time, 'in the past two centuries Britain has been in the frontline of plots and treachery against Islam and Muslims'.[5] And the deal done in 1998 by the British Foreign Secretary, Robin Cook, to re-establish relations with Iran was, in reality, a capitulation, accepting the Iranians' right to call for the murder of a British citizen by other British citizens as if it were not in the least bit troubling.

The feeble, cowardly reaction to the Rushdie fatwa marks the moment when the reality of the threat to civilized Western values became obvious, because it was now clear that the response would not be resolve but pusillanimity.

Osama bin Laden himself has compared the 'strong horse' of Islam with the 'weak horse' of the West. The ineffectual, gutless response of the British political classes to the fatwa revealed a dangerous weakness at the core of British society – a refusal to confront and take on a threat to the very norms of liberal democracy. Book burnings in the streets and repeated calls for Rushdie's murder were not merely tolerated; instead of being prosecuted, those responsible were welcomed into the bosom of the establishment. Iqbal Sacranie, for example, who led the protests and said that death was 'too good' for Rushdie, was punished with a knighthood for his services to community relations after his time at the helm of the Muslim Council of Britain. As for prosecuting for incitement those involved in protests calling for the murder of Rushdie, the idea was dismissed out of hand by the authorities, which argued that this would damage community relations. As if demanding the murder of someone for daring to insult Islam would not! By 2007, such was the moral inversion that had set in that the government was going as a supplicant to some of those very protesters, who had morphed into pillars of the Muslim Council of Britain, and offering them legislation to make criticism of Islam a criminal offence.

Yet even some of those who have now made clear that they have changed their minds over their stance on the Rushdie fatwa still see it as a boon. Inayat Bunglawala, spokesperson for the Muslim Council of Britain, described himself as being 'elated' when Khomeini issued the fatwa. Looking back in January 2009, he remarked that: 'It was a very welcome reminder that British Muslims did not have to regard themselves just as a small, vulnerable minority; they were part of a truly global and powerful movement . . . It was a seminal moment in British Muslim history . . . It brought Muslims together. Before that they had been identified as ethnic communities but *The Satanic Verses* brought them together and helped develop a British Muslim identity, which I'm sure infuriates Salman Rushdie.'[6]

Worse still, the establishment is in denial over the very basic nature of the threat, retreating from truth and taking cover in liberal pieties. The sheer distortion, for instance, of the BBC's reporting of the London bombings on 7 July 2005 was breathtaking. In the immediate moments after the bombings, the murderers were, rightly, described by BBC reporters as terrorists. The BBC's website had a page with the headline BUS MAN MAY HAVE SEEN TER-RORIST. The story began: 'A bus passenger says he may have seen one of those responsible for the terrorist bomb attacks in London.' Another page referred to 'the worst terrorist atrocity Britain has seen'. The use of the word 'terrorist' was surprising but welcome – surprising because in its coverage of terrorism in Israel the BBC has consistently described the suicide murderers who blow up buses, with the specific intent of killing as many Israelis as possible, as 'extremists' or 'militants'. The word 'terrorist' never passes correspondents' lips. So to see the BBC describe the 7/7 murderers as terrorists looked like a rare example of the corporation using the appropriate term. By the following day, however, the BBC had returned to form and the webpages had been edited to excise all references to terrorism. The first page had a new headline: PASSENGER BELIEVES HE SAW BOMBER. The story was changed to: 'A bus passenger says he may have seen one of those responsible for the bomb attacks in London.' And the second story mentioned 'the worst peacetime bomb attacks Britain has seen'. No mention of terrorism was anywhere to be seen.

But those edits affected merely the BBC's own words. What the corporation did to the Prime Minister's words in his statement to the House of Commons, however, was breathtaking. Tony Blair told MPs this: 'It seems probable that the attack was carried out by Islamist extremist terrorists . . .' The BBC's report of the statement was a wilful distortion: 'Those responsible . . . probably Islamic extremists, would be hunted down.' The Prime Minister referred to them specifically as terrorists but the BBC deliberately left out that most important word. And it did not even report Mr Blair's conclusion: 'Together, we will ensure that though terrorists can kill, they will never destroy the way of life we share and which we value, and which we will defend with the strength of belief and conviction so that it is to us and not to the terrorists, that victory will belong.' There were, presumably, simply too many references to terrorists for the BBC to concoct even a distorted report.

In the BBC mindset, the murderers were not terrorists. As its Editorial Guidelines put it: 'Our credibility is undermined by the careless use of words which carry emotional or value judgements. The word "terrorist" itself can be a barrier rather than an aid to understanding.' The 'bombers' merely had a different worldview from the rest of us. Indeed, the guidelines say: 'we recognise our duty to protect the vulnerable and avoid unjustified offence or likely harm. We aim to achieve this by ensuring our output is not used to denigrate the beliefs of others.' How awful it would be if mass-murdering Islamists were offended or denigrated by being called terrorists. But terrorism is not a value judgement. It is recognized as a crime against humanity under international law. To describe the 7/7 bombers as terrorists is merely to observe human rights law.

This is, of course, about far more than labels. The refusal to use the word 'terrorist' reflects the worldview of so many in the British chattering classes, in which such murders are simply a response to the West's provocation. Frank Gardner, the BBC's Security Correspondent, has been lauded for his return to work after being shot by terrorists – excuse me, militants – in Saudi Arabia. His undoubted bravery ought, however, not to prevent his analysis of the events of 7/7 from being exposed for what it was. Speaking on BBC Radio 4 on the Monday afterwards, Gardner declared that Western policies in Muslim countries and 'harassment' of suspected Islamists in Britain and Europe were 'offensive' to the Wahhabi Muslims behind the murders. But what Wahhabis find offensive is the very existence of the West, which they are committed to destroying. Gardner then remarked that it was extraordinary that they had planted a bomb in Edgware Road since this was a Muslim area. Yet not only did they not plant a bomb there – it went off in a moving train – they also have as long a track record of murdering Muslims as they do of killing apostates. Mr Gardner concluded that it was 'doubly tough for Britain's Muslims . . . it's more of a blow for them than for everyone else'.[7] Really? The relatives and friends of the victims might disagree with that.

There was a further stark demonstration in September 2005 of the refusal of the establishment to acknowledge the reality of the threat to Western values, and its weakness in response. The reaction to the protests over the publication of some cartoons in the Danish newspaper *Jyllands-Posten* was limp to the point of being non-existent. Even after the events of 9/11, even after the Madrid bombings, even after the London bombings, the need to stand up to the threat posed by militant Islam was still not fully comprehended. The cartoons – there were a dozen in all – were not very funny and were clearly insulting, which is, after all, what they were meant to be. The cartoons had been intended as a deliberate challenge. A biographer of Mohammed had lamented the fact that artists were too intimidated to illustrate his book and the newspaper had called for cartoonists who would be willing to have their pictures published. But the response of the protesters shows precisely what was –

and is – at stake. If free speech means anything, it surely includes the ability to question and to mock the belief that Mohammed rewards jihadists, just as it must also include the freedom to stage *Jerry Springer – The Opera*, which was the subject of protests by Christians, and to perform the play *Dishonour* at the Birmingham Rep, against which Sikhs protested in 2005.

In one cartoon, Mohammed cries out to dead suicide bombers waiting to be admitted to paradise: 'Stop, stop! We ran out of virgins.' Another had him wearing a bomb. Within days the issue had gone worldwide, after Danish Muslim groups organized a series of protests – mostly violent – and the cartoons were reprinted, in an act of solidarity for free speech, in over fifty other countries. Not one British newspaper, however, saw fit to publish them, craven as the rest of the British establishment.

The Danish flag was burned across the Middle East. But the streets of Britain also saw violent protests, especially outside the Danish Embassy in Knightsbridge. Protesters dressed up as suicide bombers, wore fatigues and carried banners with calls to kill the non-believers who had insulted Islam. In response to such flagrant criminality there was not one prosecution, just timidity. And far from the Muslim Council of Britain condemning such behaviour, it joined in on the act, issuing a press release which condemned instead 'the continuing refusal of newspapers in Denmark and Norway to apologise for printing a series of sacrilegious cartoons vilifying the Prophet Mohammed'.

But Europe is not part of the Caliphate, whatever some extremists wish. One of the defining qualities of Western civilization is that, while religions of all kinds are tolerated, their beliefs and practices are subject to secular laws. The idea that any religion should be above those laws is anathema to the West. But instead of fighting to defend these principles, the British government has responded by caving in. The Danish Prime Minister, Anders Fogh Rasmussen, stood firm in his defence of free speech after ambassadors from ten Muslim countries complained to him about the cartoons. As he put it: 'The government can in no way influence the media.'[8] The British government, however, introduced the Racial and Religious Hatred Act, which ensures that it is no longer just *Satanic Verses-* or Danish cartoon-style protesters who try to silence critics but the British state itself, which now has the power to lock up those who dare to mock Mohammed.

No other religion's communal body demanded such a law. Not the Synod of the Church of England, nor the Board of Deputies of British Jews, nor Catholics, nor Sikhs, nor Hindus. The Muslim Council of Britain had, however, been lobbying for such a law since its inception in 1997 and first got its way in November 2001, with a clause in the Anti-Terrorism, Crime and Security Bill outlawing incitement to religious hatred, explicitly included as a sop to the MCB to buy its acquiescence in the passing of legislation aimed at defeating terrorism. As if there could ever be the need to gain acceptance for such a purpose!

The Muslim Council of Britain is at the heart of the problem in Britain today, representing almost everything that is wrong with the authorities' response to the threat of militant Islam. The MCB was created in the 1990s, urged on by the then Home Secretary, Michael Howard, in order to provide the government with a point of contact with the

Muslim community. It is now an umbrella group for around 400 mosques and other Muslim organizations and claims to be 'the most forceful, most reasonable and most representative spokesperson for the British Muslim community'. Whether those claims are true or not, the fact is that the MCB has been lamentable in its response to the rise of militant Islamism. Not surprising, given that it has strong associations with the hardline Jamaat-e-Islami – the sister party of the Islamist Muslim Brotherhood. The MCB is, at best, in denial about the extremism being bred in the Muslim community. It has links to Jamiat Ahl-e-Hadith, which has forty-one branches in Britain. The Jamiat Ahl-e-Hadith website proclaims: 'The disbelievers are misguided and their ways based on sick or deviant views concerning their societies, their universe and their very existence.'

At worst, the MCB is part of the problem. Take its reaction to a survey carried out in 2005 by Channel 4, which found that 51 per cent of young British Muslims thought that 9/11 was a plot by Americans and Jews, 31 per cent agreed that 7/7 was justified because of Britain's support for the war on terror and 36 per cent of all British Muslims thought that Princess Diana was killed by the state to stop her marrying a Muslim. Instead of working to correct such views, the MCB has made things worse by its leaders' repeated habit of appearing to condone almost any statement by any Muslim, however outrageous. In 1996, the extremist group Al-Mujahiroun invited Osama bin Laden to Britain to attend a 'Rally for Revival'. The Board of Deputies of British Jews condemned the move but the MCB's former secretary general, Sir Iqbal Sacranie, responded with the following comment: 'The Board of

Deputies of British Jews should seriously consider what action they take on this matter because of the detrimental effect on community relations which could result. Taking a hostile view towards scholars who wish to come to this country to present their points of view at a conference will not serve good community relations.'[9]

In an interview on the BBC's *Panorama* in 2005, Sacranie repeatedly refused to condemn Ahl-e-Hadith, which believes that 'imitating the Kuffar [non-Muslims] leads to a permanent abode in hellfire'.[10] His response was that 'we must accept the reality' of diversity within the Muslim community in the UK. Sacranie was at that time a trustee of a group called the Union of Good, chaired by Sheikh Yusuf al-Qaradawi, who believes that: 'We must plant the love of death in the Islamic nation.'[11] Al-Qaradawi is the man who was repeatedly fawned over by Ken Livingstone in his time as Mayor of London. Mr Livingstone proudly hugged him in public. Al-Qaradawi is a leading member of the Muslim Brotherhood. His fatwas influence its millions of followers. In a sermon delivered in March 2003 he instructed his followers thus: 'O God, destroy the Zionist, the American, and the British aggressors.'[12] In his weekly Al-Jazeera programme he explained that a person engaged in jihad 'is not a suicide [bomber]. He kills the enemy while taking self-risk . . . He wants to scare his enemies, and the religious authorities have permitted this.'[13] In an interview last year he said that Islam justifies suicide bombings in Iraq against the US military and in Israel against women and children. His praise for suicide murders – 'Hamas Operations are Jihad and Those Who [Carry it Out and] are Killed are

Considered Martyrs' – appears on a website linked to the terrorist group Hamas.

After the Madrid bombing in March 2004, the MCB appealed to all British Islamic organizations to 'liaise with the local police and give them the fullest co-operation with any criminal activity, including the terrorist threat'.[14] But their own actions were rather different. The East London Mosque's then chairman, Dr Muhammad Abdul Bari, who later succeeded Sacranie as head of the MCB, joined Inayat Bunglawala, the MCB's press spokesman and assistant secretary general, in signing up to a 'Stop the Political Terror' campaign, which threatened a boycott of the police and government if 'human rights abuses' by the 'British Anti-Terrorist Police' did not stop.

As Sir Salman Rushdie put it in reaction to Sacranie's knighthood in 2005: 'If Sir Iqbal Sacranie is the best [Tony] Blair can offer in the way of a good Muslim, we have a problem.'[15]

Inayat Bunglawala is another interesting character, a regular across the media in his role as a supposedly moderate voice. Bunglawala believes that the BBC and the rest of the media are controlled by Jews: 'The chairman of Carlton Communications is Michael Green of the Tribe of Judah. He has joined an elite club whose members include fellow Jews Michael Grade and Alan Yentob . . . [They are] close friends . . . so that's what they mean by a "free media".'[16] Mr Bunglawala also has a long history of support for extremists. In January 1993, he wrote a letter to *Private Eye* in which he described Sheikh Omar Abdul Rahman as 'courageous' – a month before the man bombed the World Trade Center in New York. When Rahman was arrested for the crime, Mr Bunglawala said that the arrest was probably only a result of his 'calling on Muslims to fulfil their duty to Allah and to fight against oppression and oppressors everywhere'. Mr Bunglawala has also distributed the words of Osama bin Laden, whom he labelled a 'freedom fighter'.[17] And, unsurprisingly, Bunglawala was an enthusiastic *Satanic Verses* book burner.

The Islamic ideology favoured by the MCB leadership is inspired by Syed Abul Ala Maududi, the originator of Islamism, which sees Islam as a political as well as a religious force, aiming to establish Sharia law across the planet. To that end, in 1941 he founded Pakistan's Jamaat-e-Islami party and influenced Sayyid Qutb, ideologue of the Muslim Brotherhood. Maududi believed that all non-Muslims are 'barbarians' and wrote that 'the aim of Islam is to bring about a universal revolution'.[18] Sacranie's successor as general secretary of the MCB, Dr Muhammad Abdul Bari, is no less distinguished in these areas. As chairman of the Saudi-funded East London Mosque, he invited Sheikh Abdul Rahman al-Sudais, imam at the Ka'ba mosque in Mecca (the most important shrine in the Muslim world), to London. The imam believes: 'Read history and you will understand that the Jews of yesterday are the evil fathers of the Jews of today, who are evil offspring, infidels, distorters of words, calf-worshippers, prophet-murderers, prophecy-deniers . . . the scum of the human race "whom Allah cursed and turned into apes and pigs . . ." These are the Jews, an ongoing continuum of deceit, obstinacy, licentiousness, evil, and corruption.'[19] This is what is described as a moderate view. In July 2006, Bari welcomed Delwar Hossain Sayeedi, a Bangladeshi MP and member of

Maududi's Jamaat-e-Islami, to the East London Mosque. Sayeedi has said that the UK and the US 'deserve all that is coming to them' for overthrowing the Taliban in Afghanistan, and has compared Bangladeshi Hindus to excrement.[20]

A perfect vignette of the slow march to collapse occurred on 22 July 2008. The BBC's website had a story headlined MUSLIM CONCERN AT STOP AND SEARCH: 'Muslims in Scotland have expressed unease about the use of "stop and search" procedures at Glasgow Airport.' There could be few things more likely to stir up anger against ordinary, peaceable Muslims than the idea that they should object to security measures against terror. But dig deeper and a very different story emerges. The Muslims expressing unease were from the Scottish Islamic Foundation, a small group which had been given a £215,000 grant by the Scottish Executive and was then exposed as a Muslim Brotherhood-linked organization, some of whose members are willing to further divisions between Muslims and non-Muslims. These SIF activists represent almost no one other than themselves. But the BBC story shows the vicious circle at work: public money has been given to an extremist group, the BBC portrays it as a voice of mainstream Muslims, the non-Muslim public reacts with anger and the activists' aim has been fulfilled, all because of our own actions.[21]

Such is the nature of the fight to defend Western values – half-hearted, supine and suicidal in the face of Islamic preachers whose vocabulary is hate and Islamic revolution. Indeed, even the Archbishop of Canterbury has embraced the adoption of Sharia law, like some satirist's caricature of a limp-wristed vicar, always doing the bidding of those who seek to subvert him and his church. Speaking to the BBC in February 2008, he said that the UK has to 'face up to the fact' that some of its citizens do not relate to the British legal system and that adopting parts of Islamic Sharia law would help maintain social cohesion. Dr Williams then said of the idea that 'there's one law for everybody . . . I think that's a bit of a danger'. One has to remind oneself that the man arguing for the adoption in legislation of Sharia law because Muslims should not have to choose between 'the stark alternatives of cultural loyalty or state loyalty'[22] is the Archbishop of Canterbury. It's a stark alternative in one sense, yes. Because there ought to be no dilemma, no debate and no choice. If one lives in the UK, one obeys UK law and no other if there is a conflict, whether one is Muslim, Jewish, Hindu, Sikh, Scientologist or whatever. As for having one law for Muslims and one law for everyone else: the 'bit of a danger' is when supposed national leaders give up the ghost of defending Western values and cave in to demands for the adoption of Sharia.

Which is exactly what they have done. Just months after the Archbishop's contribution to the defence of Western civilization, the government quietly sanctioned the right of Sharia courts in London, Birmingham, Bradford, Manchester and Nuneaton to have their rulings enforced with the full power of the judicial system. Instead of relying on voluntary compliance, a perfectly valid practice, Sharia law has now, in part, been incorporated into the law of the land. As the *Daily Telegraph* reported: 'Muslim tribunal courts started passing sharia judgments in August

2007. They have dealt with more than 100 cases that range from Muslim divorce and inheritance to nuisance neighbours. It has also emerged that tribunal courts have settled six cases of domestic violence between married couples, working in tandem with the police investigations. Sheikh Faiz-ul-Aqtab Siddiqi, whose Muslim Arbitration Tribunal runs the courts, said that sharia courts are classified as arbitration tribunals under a clause in the Arbitration Act 1996.'[23] And what were some of the first judgements handed down?

> Mr Siddiqi said that in a recent inheritance dispute handled by the court in Nuneaton, the estate of a Midlands man was divided between three daughters and two sons. The judges on the panel gave the sons twice as much as the daughters, in accordance with sharia. Had the family gone to a normal British court, the daughters would have got equal amounts. In the six cases of domestic violence, Mr Siddiqi said the judges ordered the husbands to take anger management classes and mentoring from community elders. There was no further punishment. In each case, the women subsequently withdrew the complaints they had lodged with the police and the police stopped their investigations.[24]

So much for gender equality under the law. So much for a government committed to acting against domestic violence.

As the expert on jihadist ideology and former Muslim Patrick Sookhdeo writes of the failure of the British establishment to confront the danger:

The whole approach towards Muslim militants was based on appeasement. 7/7 proved that that approach does not work – yet it is still being followed. For example, there is a book, *The Noble Koran: a New Rendering of its Meaning in English*, which is openly available in Muslim bookshops. It calls for the killing of Jews and Christians, and it sets out a strategy for killing the infidels and for warfare against them. The Government has done nothing whatever to interfere with the sale of that book. Why not? Government ministers have promised to punish religious hatred, to criminalise the glorification of terrorism, yet they do nothing about this book, which blatantly does both . . . The trouble is that . . . [they] see Islam through the prism of their own secular outlook. They simply do not realise how seriously Muslims take their religion. Islamic clerics regard themselves as locked in mortal combat with secularism. For example, one of the fundamental notions of a secular society is the moral importance of freedom, of individual choice. But in Islam, choice is not allowable: there cannot be free choice about whether to choose or reject any of the fundamental aspects of the religion, because they are all divinely ordained. God has laid down the law, and man must obey.[25]

But it is no wonder that the Archbishop and government can come out with such suicidal ideas as enshrining Sharia under the law, when the officials employed to advise the authorities on such issues are themselves part of the problem. Take the Foreign and Commonwealth Office for example, which, far from fighting threats to liberal democracy, has engaged in classic appeasement, supporting the activities of Islamists dedicated to the destruction of Western society: the FCO actively promotes engagement with the likes of the Muslim Brotherhood and its associated groups. Mockbul Ali, the FCO's Islamic Issues adviser, pressed for the granting of entry visas to Yusuf al-Qaradawi and Delwar Hossain Sayeedi, despite the latter's visits to the UK usually being accompanied by violence. To Mockbul Ali, Sayeedi is a 'mainstream' figure. Mr Ali's views, based on the supposed merits of 'engagement', are now standard within the FCO. His colleague Angus McKee has even proposed direct funding of groups dedicated to wiping out Western civilization: 'Given that Islamist groups are often less corrupt than the generality of the societies in which they operate, consideration might be given to channelling aid resources through them, so long as sufficient transparency is achievable.'[26]

A perfect example of how militant Islam operates is the IslamExpo exhibition which took place in Olympia in July 2008. It was, the organizers maintained: 'Europe's largest celebration of Islamic culture, tradition, innovation and art'. IslamExpo is the brainchild of Mohammed Sawalha, the President of the British Muslim Initiative. The BBC's *Panorama* reported in 2006 that, according to some of its sources, Mr Sawalha 'masterminded much of Hamas's political and military strategy' and in London 'is alleged to have directed funds, both for Hamas' armed wing, and for spreading its missionary *dawah*'.

The tactic is simple. Hamas and the Muslim Brotherhood are pushing the notion that there are two types of Islamism – moderate and extreme. They represent, they would have us believe, the moderates. IslamExpo had all sorts of peaceable, fun and unthreatening activities: art, football and lovely food. The FCO-funded British Satellite News pushed a gushing image of IslamExpo for overseas viewers. But if that was not enough to persuade us of the sense of allying with moderate Islamists, there was always an implicit threat underneath the guff. If we don't throw in our lot with them, we'll be left only with the real extremists: Al Qaeda. But Hamas and the Muslim Brotherhood are not an ally against extremism; they *are* the extremists.

Deluded engagement with those whose existence is dedicated to destroying our society is par for the FCO course. As Halifax wrote to Eden in 1937: 'I went to see the PM. He was very strong that I ought to manage to see Hitler . . . He truly observed that we might as well get all the contact we could.' Did we not learn in the 1930s the consequences of such contact with those who seek to destroy us?

10

THE FAMILY

24 October 1970

On 24 October 1970 *The Female Eunuch* was published, written by Germaine Greer, a young Australian academic. The book's central argument was simple, if controversial: that women do not realize how much men hate them and how much they are taught to hate themselves. Its publication was a sensation and turned Greer into an international superstar.

Germaine Greer was born in Melbourne on 29 January 1939. She was brought up in a well-to-do family (her mother, Margaret, had been a milliner's apprentice and then model before becoming a housewife and her father, Reg, was the Melbourne advertising salesman for an Adelaide-based newspaper group) and educated at a private convent school, Star of the Sea College. In 1959, she began a degree in English and French at Melbourne University. Moving afterwards to Sydney, she lectured at the city's university while studying for an MA in Romantic poetry, for which in 1963 she was awarded a first for her thesis on Byron. The following year she won a Commonwealth Scholarship and arrived at Newnham College, Cambridge, to begin her doctorate.

In Sydney she had fallen in with the so-called 'Sydney Push', a group of polygamous anarchists. As Greer's biographer, Christine Wallace, puts it:

> For Germaine, [the Push] provided a philosophy to underpin the attitude and lifestyle she had already acquired in Melbourne. She walked into the Royal George Hotel, into the throng talking themselves hoarse in a room stinking of stale beer and thick with cigarette smoke, and set out to follow the Push way of life – 'an intolerably difficult discipline which I forced myself to learn'. The Push struck her as completely different from the Melbourne intelligentsia she had engaged with . . . these people talked about truth and only truth, insisting that most of what we were exposed to during the day was ideology, which was a synonym for lies – or bullshit, as they called it.' Her Damascus turned out to be the Royal George . . . 'I was already an anarchist,' she says. 'I just didn't know why I was an anarchist. They put me in touch with the basic texts and I found out what the internal logic was about how I felt and thought.'[1]

Greer was a striking presence who seemed constitutionally incapable of failing to make a stir, wherever she was. One of her fellow students at Newnham was Lisa Jardine, who recalled her first sighting of Greer:

> Germaine Greer first impinged on my own life in my final year as an undergraduate at Newnham College, Cambridge. We women students were all gathered together in the college hall for the annual Founders' Day Feast, and as we finished eating, the principal called us to order for the speeches. As a hush descended, one person continued to speak, too engrossed in her conversation to notice, her strong Australian voice reverberating round the room.
>
> At the graduates' table, Germaine was explaining with passion that there could be no liberation for women, no matter how highly educated, as long as we were required to cram our breasts into bras constructed like mini-Vesuviuses, two stitched, white, cantilevered cones which bore no resemblance to the female anatomy. The willingly suffered discomfort of the Sixties bra, she opined vigorously, was a hideous symbol of male oppression.
>
> I'd like to be able to recall that we hallooed and thumped the tables, or that we erupted into a spontaneous roar of approval, a guffaw of sisterly laughter. We should have done, but we didn't. We were too astonished at the very idea that a woman could speak so loudly and out of turn, and that words such as 'bra' and 'breasts' (or maybe she said 'tits') could be uttered amid the pseudo-masculine solemnity of a college dinner. I am embarrassed to remember how sheltered we were then, how closed our vocabularies and our minds.

Four years later, in 1970, *The Female Eunuch* changed all that.[2]

Greer was awarded her PhD (for a thesis on 'The Ethic of Love and Marriage in Shakespeare's Early Comedies') in 1968 and moved to Warwick University to lecture in English. But she had already started to be active beyond academic life. At Cambridge she had joined the Footlights and under the pseudonym Rose Blight she wrote a gardening column for *Private Eye*. She was also a regular contributor to *Oz* magazine (which in 1971 was prosecuted for obscenity in an infamous trial). She posed nude for the magazine and edited an issue in July 1970 in which she also wrote an article on the hand-knitted Cock Sock, 'a snug corner for a chilly prick'.

But although her name was beginning to be recognized by habitués of the London media scene, Greer's breakthrough – something of an understatement – came with the publication of *The Female Eunuch* in October 1970, when she was thirty-one. The book was not just an instant bestseller (within six months it had sold out its second printing and been translated into eight languages); it was an instant staple of debate. So huge was the controversy it engendered that no one seemed to be without an opinion on it, and few of those were not at one extreme or the other.

Greer's book now seems slightly passé; we are long used to hearing such things. But in 1970 her arguments were deeply shocking, the first time such feminist thoughts had been given a mainstream hearing. The central tenet of the book was that the traditional family was damaging to both women and children. Right from the start, according to Greer, girls are subjugated by being taught supposedly female behaviour which is, in reality, nothing more than a male device for keeping them in check. As they grow into adulthood and adopt the stereotypical version of femininity, they become ashamed of their bodies and lose their natural self: 'The ignorance and isolation of most women mean that they are incapable of making conversation: most of their communication with their spouses is a continuation of the power struggle. The result is that when wives come along to dinner parties they pervert civilised conversation about real issues into personal quarrels. The number of hostesses who wish they did not have to invite wives is legion.'[3]

To change this unnatural and oppressive state of affairs, Greer argued that women should not only get to know their bodies but should also lose the ridiculous, male-imposed adherence to monogamy – and should, as part of getting to know their bodies better, drink their menstrual blood. As Greer put it in an interview at the time: 'The title is an indication of the problem. Women have somehow been separated from their libido, from their faculty of desire, from their sexuality. They've become suspicious about it. Like beasts, for example, who are castrated in farming in order to serve their master's ulterior motives – to be fattened or made docile – women have been cut off from their capacity for action. It's a process that sacrifices vigour for delicacy and succulence, and one that's got to be changed.'[4]

Unlike earlier feminist tracts, *The Female Eunuch* was actually a good read. It hectored its reader, yes, but it was by turns witty, angry and trenchantly readable, which lifted it beyond the narrow academic and feminist confines of previous screeds. And its reach was overwhelming. As Professor Lisa Jardine writes:

> Every self-respecting woman on the Left owned a copy – still owns a copy – somewhere around the house, dog-eared and coffee-stained with use. Greer's detractors may pooh-pooh its influence, but the fact is that for women born in the immediate postwar years there was 'before Greer' and 'after Greer'. The book, and Germaine's attention-grabbing brand of stand-up-comic, in-your-face assertiveness, taught us all how to behave badly and take control of our lives. She was Mae West, Dorothy Parker and Gertrude Stein rolled into one, with a touch of the self-parodying Lenny Henrys. Her epoch-making book had an enduring impact because it and she were outrageous, bad and dangerous, and, above all, hilariously funny. And all you girl-power grrrrls out there who claim you never read her, so she didn't make a difference for you, can stop kidding your-selves. You are standing on her statuesque shoulders; she did it first.[5]

Greer was not universally popular within the feminist movement, and not just because others were jealous of her phenomenal success. Her biographer describes her as a sexual liberationist first and a feminist second. Her mes-sage, after all, was that the sexual repression of women (the female eunuch) destroys the energy and life they need to break free of male bonds, and that the means to that freedom is sexual liberation. As she wrote: 'You see, the group f*** is the highest ritual expression of our faith.' It was no wonder that *Life* magazine referred to her in an explanation for its readers of the book's success as 'a saucy feminist that even men like'. Her brand of feminist was not the dungaree-clad, man-hating monster of legend; rather, her antics might almost have been designed to titillate men, as she stripped off at every opportunity.

She was also keen to be frank about her sexual exploits and to condemn those who did not match up to her expectations. In one piece published just before *The Female Eunuch*, Greer wrote about being 'In Bed with the English', in which she detailed her rotten experience with English lovers. The article was a red rag to the 1960s English bull. Peter Cook publicly burned the article and another reader suggested that Ms Greer try him out as a corrective: 'An Englishman, if good, is the best lover in the world. Germaine must be pretty ugly or a raving nympho trying too hard.'

Clearly, one book did not change an entire social structure. But *The Female Eunuch* was, in a sense, the right book for the right time. Greer's ideas were not new; they were a variation on the much-debated feminist themes of the 1960s. Greer's real contribution was to push the ideas beyond a narrow audience and into the mainstream, and to do this at a time when baby-boomers were on the rise and receptive to ideas which appeared to give intellectual and ideological justification to their instinctive self-centredness.

The legacy of the baby-boomer generation – loosely defined as those born between the end of the Second World War and the early 1960s – is with us today, in the impact of the social revolution it pursued. (The UK baby boom was at its peak in 1947, when more babies were born than in any other year since 1920.) The baby-boomers effectively rebuilt Western civilization in the mould of the 1960s culture of social revolt. Whatever had been traditionally regarded as the glue of society was, by definition, held to be wrong and stifling. If marriage was the bedrock, it was archaic. If children were traditionally born with two ever-present parents, then, rather, one-parent families were a woman's right. Anything that stifled the immediate gratification of desire was viewed as a shackle of the past which had to be lifted. *The Female Eunuch* went far beyond feminism in its impact. It gave apparent intellectual and historical justification for putting the self first as a release from crippling restraints and putting the individual's rights above those of the community, which by definition was repressive.

But what made the baby-boomer generation uniquely able to change society was that it could, unlike any previous generation, indulge its every whim and act entirely without constraint. Born into a long period of unusual peace and security, the baby-boomers were able to benefit from the post-war era's prosperity and full employment. It seemed as if the world were an unending source of wish-fulfilment, with economic growth running hand in hand with amazing scientific breakthroughs – not the least of which was the Pill. Even unwanted pregnancy was now defeated. Sex, it was said, carried no risks and should be treated as nothing more than a form of self-fulfilment, or even as entertainment. And unlike their hidebound predecessors, the baby-boomers knew – they were nothing if not self-possessed – that they were the most rounded, intelligent and self-aware generation in history. They knew that what was best for them was best for everyone else. They knew that self-expression led to the flowering of human potential. And they knew that personal fulfilment was now not just possible; it was critical for the betterment of society.

They might have thought all that. But they knew in fact nothing of the sort, because the evidence shows that they were as wrong as it is possible to be. All their ideals amounted to, as we will see, was putting the individual's short-term desires above any longer-term, wider impact on others.

Take the impact on the family. The single most destructive social problem of our time is the progressive disintegration of the family, which has not only caused untold direct misery and harm but has also had profound consequences on areas such as education and crime. *Breakdown Britain*, an exhaustive report by the former leader of the Conservative Party, Iain Duncan Smith, calculated that disintegrating families and their social consequences cost £20 billion a year, in part through the cost of government support programmes and the decreased tax revenue caused by poverty among single-mother households. Researchers using data from the National Child Development Study provide a telling insight into the reality of family breakdown, showing that children whose parents split up are more likely to end up without qualifications, claiming benefits and suffering depression. In 1960, 90 per cent of children were still living with both their parents at the age of 16. As the divorce rate grew, this fell to 79 per cent for those born in the 1970s. Today, a third of children experience the separation or divorce of their parents before the age of 16. It might be a reasonable assumption that the increased prevalence of divorce would mean it had a steadily less deleterious impact on children; as parental splits became more normal, so there would be less stigma and less impact. A reasonable assumption, perhaps, but an entirely wrong one. The impact remains just as devastating as ever. As the researchers put it: 'The estimates across cohorts are surprisingly similar in magnitude and not significantly different from one another.' Divorce 'has repercussions that reverberate through childhood and into adulthood . . . Children from disrupted families tend to do less well in school and subsequent careers than their peers. They are also more likely to experience the break-up of their own partnerships.'[6]

It is not just divorce that has an impact. The Millennium Cohort Study found that cohabiting couples were more than twice as likely to split up as married couples, regardless of age, income or social background. Even the poorest 20 per cent of married couples are more stable than the richest 20 per cent of cohabiting couples, according to the *Breakdown Britain* report. In 1971, 68 per cent of the population were married. By 2001 that had fallen to 54 per cent and it is projected to decline to 41 per cent in 2031. Indeed, the latest statistics on births within marriage reveal a transformation within British society. In Chapter One, we saw how one in five babies is now born to a foreign mother (one in two in London). But beneath that bald figure lies a fascinating change. Immigrants now conform better than native Britons to what are usually thought of as 'traditional' British values: far more children of immigrants are born within marriage than of native Britons. If immigrants are ignored, 2007 was the first year in recorded history in which more children were born outside than inside marriage in the UK.[7] Britain leads the European lone-parent league by a long way. Fifteen per cent of all children in Britain are now born and brought up without a father. In 2005, nearly one in four dependent children in Britain – 3.2 million – was living in a lone-parent family.

Why does this matter? Whatever we might want to believe, the statistics show clearly that children from single-parent households are exponentially more likely than those in intact families to suffer deprivation and ill-health, to get into trouble at school, to suffer physical and sexual abuse, to drink, to take drugs, to commit crime, to contract sexually transmitted diseases, to become teenage parents – and, at the most basic level, to be poor as adults. Official statistics show that some 70 per cent of young criminal offenders come from lone-parent families. Children growing up in lone-parent families are twice as likely to suffer a mental disorder as those living with married parents. And the rising number of lone-parent families is one of the biggest reasons for housing shortages. Ninety-five per cent of lone-parent families receive benefits or tax credits, with 45 per cent claiming housing benefit. Britain has the highest rates of benefits for single mothers and the highest percentage of lone-parent families in Europe. Cause and effect, perhaps?

Every year, over 47,000 girls under 18 fall pregnant, the highest number (per head of the population) in Western Europe: six times that of Holland, four times that of Italy and three times higher than in France. And, for good measure, we also have the highest number of school-age abortions. Of girls aged under 16 – the age of consent – 13.8 per cent are now infected with chlamydia. Even after they have been treated, 28 per cent become reinfected within 6 months and 20 per cent within a year. Even serious disease seems not to act as a warning against promiscuity. Is it any wonder? The notion that sex is just another form of entertainment is now so widespread, whether through gossipy media stories of which celebrity is shagging which other celebrity, or even through school, where sex education and the emphasis on contraception carry with them the implication that having sex is fine so long as one takes care. The intended message might be that when children have sex they should use a condom, but the only part which seems to get through is the 'when children have sex' part.

For years, politicians shied away from even acknowledging, letting alone tackling, the consequences of family break-up. Hardly surprising: the few who did mention it were often caught out as hypocrites. Even John Major, who was so wild that he ran away from the circus to become an accountant, was eventually revealed to have had an affair. But the baby-boomer generation which grew to maturity in the 1960s and which still carried the decade's baggage could hardly have tackled these issues without acknowledging the fundamental errors of its outlook and its responsibility for these changes in society.

It has only been with the rise to pre-eminence of a generation which has had to suffer the consequences of its predecessors' behaviour that the family has been accepted as something more than an annoying constriction on self-fulfilment. In 2007, David Cameron, the ultra-modernizing Conservative, showed how the wheel was beginning to turn full circle: 'I'll tell you what's wrong,' Cameron said in a speech. 'We have too many children behaving like adults and too many adults behaving like children ... If we are to rebuild our broken society we have to get the foundation right. And the foundation of society is – or should be – the care of children by the man and the woman who brought them into the world.' He wanted, he said, to see 'more couples stay together, and we know the best way to ensure this is to support marriage'.[8]

It is not just children who suffer. Lone parents are poorer, more depressed and less healthy than their married counterparts; and separated fathers drink more heavily, have more unsafe sex and suffer higher death rates. Meanwhile, the old are turfed out of care homes that are forced to close and no longer have families to look after them. If there is such a thing as society, the family is its foundation. A breakdown in the family causes a breakdown in society.

The baby-boomers might have changed society but the consequences of their behaviour were made far more potent by the impact of the Beveridge Report. Paradoxically, Lord Beveridge's report of December 1942 sought to bolster family life for the poor through the introduction of a 'cradle to the grave' welfare state. In that respect, it was a perfect example of one of the golden rules of public policy – the law of unintended consequences. Far from protecting family life, the welfare state has helped to destroy the very purpose of families. When the state provides education, health care, old people's homes and unemployment support, what is left for the family to do? Why bother with familial obligations? If self-expression and self-fulfilment are the be-all and end-all of life, why be shackled by the family? A report in 2006 by the Centre for Monetary and Financial Studies in Madrid clarified this process, finding that high unemployment benefits and the ease with which applicants can qualify for them led to the unemployed in the UK being far less dependent on the family than elsewhere. The report found that the British are the least likely in Europe to live near relatives, share a home with family members or have older children living at home. Families in Spain are three times more likely to have a son or daughter over twenty-five living at home than in Britain. In Italy, the unemployed people are nine times more likely to be helped by their relations than in Britain, where only one in a hundred receives family assistance. Professor Samuel Bentolila, who led the research, found that: 'One possibility is that those [family] networks may have been weakened by the generosity of the welfare state in Britain.'[9]

The Beveridge Report's heart was certainly in the right place but the downside of the system which Beveridge designed now far outweighs any merits. The NHS itself is a cash-guzzler which is incapable of fulfilling its aims, being inherently flawed, designed for an age when command and control and open rationing were the norm, and largely responsible for Britain's shameful health-care record. The benefit system bequeathed by Beveridge causes welfare dependency. This welfare system destroyed the once typically British and thriving charitable sector and notions of self-reliance and self-help.

None of this is inevitable. Countries such as Denmark, Sweden and the United States have stared at the precipice and pulled back. Their statistics are now on a steady curve of improvement. Despite warnings from the so-called 'poverty lobby' that President Clinton's welfare reforms, imposing rigid limits on benefit entitlements and deadlines for the ending of welfare payments, would lead to families starving and children dying in the streets, the reality was staggering in its beneficial impact. For fifty years, welfare rolls had grown. Within five years of Clinton's reforms, caseloads had dropped by at least 60 per cent. In some states, dole queues were cut by up to 80 per cent. Teen pregnancy rates – for all races – are lower. And even though there has been an overall increase in single-parent families, the birth rate among unmarried teens fell to its lowest level since the late 1980s.

For three decades, Britain has suffered from a collapse in the family. The impact has been devastating across so many areas. Some politicians and opinion-formers are beginning to realize what is happening, and that something can be done. David Cameron has made social reform and the family cornerstones of his policies. Within Labour, too, there is a greater realization among the generation after the baby-boomers that something has to change. There will still be those who claim that everything is for the best in this best of all possible worlds, but overwhelmingly they will be from that very baby-boomer generation which has been responsible for the mess. Now that a new generation is rising to prominence, at last the tide may turn.

NOTES

1: IMMIGRATION

1 Mike Phillips and Trevor Phillips, *Windrush* (HarperCollins, 1998), p. 47
2 Tony Sewell, *Keep On Moving* (Voice, 1998), p. 18
3 PRO CO 876/88
4 Sewell, op. cit., p. 21
5 Ibid., p. 18
6 Ibid., p. 19
7 PRO LAB 8/1816
8 PRO CO 876/88
9 Phillips and Phillips, op. cit., p. 67
10 Sewell, op. cit., p. 19
11 *South London Press*, 25 June 1948
12 Phillips and Phillips, op. cit., p. 86
13 Ibid., p. 88
14 Parliamentary Debates (Commons) 453, 7 July 1948
15 Phillips and Phillips, op. cit., p. 75
16 Quoted in *Daily Telegraph*, 5 August 2007
17 W. Cunningham in C. Wilson, ed., *Alien Immigrants to England* (Frank Cass, 1969), p. 255
18 *Population Trends* number 118, Winter 2004, p. 11
19 'Foreign-born', ONS, 15 December 2005
20 'Population change', ONS, 24 August 2006

21 *The Times*, 23 August 2007
22 R. Winder, *Bloody Foreigners – the Story of Immigration to Britain* (Little, Brown, 2004), p. 321
23 *The Times*, 23 August 2007
24 *Sunday Telegraph*, 10 December 2007

2: THE ARTS

1 F.M. Leventhal, 'The Best for the Most: CEMA and State Sponsorship of the Arts in Wartime, 1939–1945', in *Twentieth Century British History*, vol. 1, no. 3 (OUP, 1990)
2 Ibid., p. 290
3 Ibid., p. 292
4 Ibid., p. 307
5 Royal Commission on Gambling, Final Report, Cmnd 7200, 1978, p. 226
6 Hansard, 25 October 1995, col. 1050
7 Mintel consumer spending report, January 1996
8 Press Association, 26 August 1995
9 http://www.camelotgroup.co.uk/socialreport2005/ strategy-and-consultation.htm
10 Andrew Adonis and Stephen Pollard, *A Class Act* (Hamish Hamilton, 1997), p. 275
11 *Daily Telegraph*, 2 July 2008
12 *Spectator*, 30 January 2008

3: EDUCATION

1
   http://www.guardian.co.uk/education/2008/jun/05/schools.publicschools
2 Robin Pedley, *The Comprehensive School* (Penguin, 1963)
3 *The Times*, leading article, 13 July 1961
4 Pedley, op. cit.

5 *Educational Priority*, DES, vol. 1 (HMSO, 1972)

6 Kevin Jefferys, *Anthony Crosland* (Richard Cohen Books, 1999), p. 100

7 Ibid., p. 103

8 Ibid.

9 Anthony Crosland, *The Future of Socialism*, 1956

10 Melanie Phillips, *All Must Have Prizes* (Little, Brown, 1996), p. 208

11 Jefferys, op. cit., p. 104

12 Ibid.

13 *The Times*, 16 November 1965

14 *Times Educational Supplement*, 1 September 1967

15 Phillips, op. cit., p. 207

16 http://www.telegraph.co.uk/news/uknews/1559452/%27Easy%27-A-levels-blamed-on-soft-courses.html

17 http://www.timesonline.co.uk/tol/news/uk/education/article3137747.ece

18 Adrian Wooldridge, *Measuring the Mind* (CUP, 1994), p. 306

19 Phillips, op. cit., p. 202

20 Ibid., p. 204

21 Ibid., p. 209

22 Ibid.

23 Ibid., p. 49

24 Ibid., p. 67

25 Ibid.

26 http://www.reform.co.uk/documents/The%20value%20of%20mathematics.pdf

27 *Guardian*, 24 June 2008

28 *Sunday Telegraph*, 7 January 1996

29 Ibid.

30 http://www.reform.co.uk/documents/The%20value%20of%20mathematics.pdf

31 Adrian Wooldridge, *Meritocracy and the Classless Society* (SMF, 1995)

32 Phillips, op. cit., p. 160
33 Ibid., p. 135
34 John Marks, *Standards in Schools* (SMF, 1991)
35 Cited in Stephen Pollard, *Schools, Standards and the Left* (SMF, 1995)

4: FOOD

1 http://www.guardian.co.uk/uk/2007/dec/30/schools. schoolmeals
2 *Daily Telegraph*, 21 March 2006
3 http://www.statistics.gov.uk/cci/nugget.asp?id=868
4 Joanna Blythman, *Bad Food Britain* (Fourth Estate, 2006), pp. xv, xvi
5 *Observer*, 9 October 2005
6 Blythman, op. cit., p. 80
7 Simon Hopkinson, *Roast Chicken and Other Stories – Second Helpings* (Macmillan, 2001)
8 http://www.3663.co.uk/gen/
9 www.foodforum.org.uk
10 'Public Perceptions of Food and Farming in Scotland', cited in *Sunday Herald*, 12 January 2003
11 Blythman, op. cit., p. 24
12 *The Grocer*, 3 April 2004
13 BBC News, 21 February 2003
14 *Guardian*, 8 June 2005
15 Nicola Humble, *Culinary Pleasures* (Faber and Faber, 2005), p. 136
16 Blythman, op. cit., p. 86
17 *The Times*, 22 February 2003
18 Blythman, op. cit., p. xv
19 www.bestofbritish.fr
20 http://archive.food.gov.uk/hea/index2.html
21 Blythman, op. cit., p. 181
22 *Guardian*, 10 September 2008

23 *Guardian*, 4 January 2005

24 Blythman, op. cit.

25 Erin Pizzey, *The Slut's Cook Book* (Macdonald, 1981), p. 146

26 Delia Smith, *How to Cheat at Cooking* (Ebury Press, 1971), p. 7

27 Pat Mainardi, *The Politics of Housework* (Redstockings, 1970)

28 Blythman, op. cit., p. 72

29 Smith, op. cit., p. 24

30 Cited by Sean French, *New Statesman*, 14 April 1995

31 Ibid.

32 http://www.timesonline.co.uk/tol/sport/columnists/martin_samuel/article590234.ece

33 Blythman, op. cit., p. 236

34 *Daily Telegraph*, 27 July 2008

35 http://www.esrcsocietytoday.ac.uk/ESRCInfoCentre/facts/index55.aspx

5: POLITICS

1 Tony Benn, *The End of an Era: Diaries 1980–90* (Hutchinson, 1992), p. 69

2 Ivor Crewe and Anthony King, *SDP: The Birth, Life and Death of the Social Democratic Party* (OUP, 1995), p. 14

3 http://www.guardian.co.uk/politics/2007/aug/04/labour.interviews

4 Crewe and King, op. cit., p. 57

5 Ibid., p. 58

6 Ibid., p. 37

7 Ibid., p. 32

8 Ibid., p. 39

9 Ibid., p. 40

10 Ibid.

11 Annual Conference Report, 1980, p. 31

12 *Sunday Times*, 30 November 1980

13 Crewe and King, op. cit., p. 89

14 Ibid., p. 92
15 Ibid., p. 94
16 *The Times*, 11 May 2005

6: THE MONARCHY

1 http://www.guardian.co.uk/media/2002/mar/05/themonarchy.
   broadcasting
2 http://members.tripod.com/~royalty09/knockout.html
3 http://www.guardian.co.uk/media/2002/mar/05/themonarchy.
   broadcasting
4 http://www.guardian.co.uk/media/2002/mar/05/themonarchy.
   broadcasting
5 http://www.guardian.co.uk/media/2002/mar/05/themonarchy.
   broadcasting
6 http://www.telegraph.co.uk/news/uknews/1358014/Prince-
   Edward-to-apologise-to-Queen-and-agrees-to-stop-making-
   royal-films.html
7 http://edition.cnn.com/2002/WORLD/europe/05/29/
   people.royals.3/

7: CRIME

1 David Fraser, *A Land Fit for Criminals* (Book Guild, 2006), p. 93
2 Ibid., p. xvi
3 Ibid.
4 http://www.telegraph.co.uk/opinion/main.jhtml;
   jsessionid=4KOYRZX3MK1TPQFIQMFSFGGAVCBQ0IV0?
   xml=/opinion/2008/01/27/do2703.xml
5 Fraser, op. cit., p. 249
6 David Green, 'Do the Official Crime Figures Tell the Full Story?'
   (Civitas, 2003)
7 Fraser, op. cit., p. 252
8 http://www.telegraph.co.uk/opinion/main.jhtml

jsessionid=4KOYRZX3MK1TPQFIQMFSFGGAVCBQ0IV0?
xml=/opinion/2008/01/27/do2703.xml

9 Jose Harris, *Private Lives, Public Spirit: Britain 1870–1914* (Penguin, 1994)

10 Peter Hitchens, *A Brief History of Crime* (Atlantic Books, 2003), p. 13

11 *Independent*, 1 February 2001

12 *Mirror*, 22 March 1995

13 Fraser, op. cit., p. 8

14 David Green, 'Forces of Law and Order Have Lost Control' (Civitas, 2002)

15 Fraser, op. cit., p. 9

16 Ibid., p. 81

17 Ibid.

18 Charles Murray et al., 'Simple Justice' (Civitas, 2005)

19 Fraser, op. cit., p. 82

20 Ibid., p. 77

21 Ibid., p. 297

22 *Sunday Telegraph*, 18 July 2008

23 Fraser, op. cit., p. 39

24 Home Office, Probation Statistics for 1998, 2000

25 Fraser, op. cit., p. 223

26 *Observer*, 1 August 1993

27 *Telegraph*, 9 October 1993

28 *Sunday Times*, 22 May 1994

29 Fraser, op. cit., p. 229

30 Home Office Statistical Bulletin, *Cautions, Court Proceedings and Sentencing*, 20/01

31 http://www.telegraph.co.uk/news/uknews/1538756/Penalty-notices-for-one-crime-in-nine.html

32 Hitchens, op. cit., p. 54

33 Ibid., p. 55

34 Ibid., p. 60

35 Ibid.

36 Ibid., p. 73

37 *Daily Mail*, 27 February 1999

38 Murray, 'Simple Justice' (Civitas, 2005)

39 Department of Health, *National Treatment Outcome Research Study*, 1998

40 Fraser, op. cit., p. 157

41 Ian Taylor, Paul Walton and Jock Young, *The New Criminology: For a Social Theory of Deviance* (Routledge, 1973)

42 Fraser, op. cit., p. 59

43 Howard Jones, *Crime in a Changing Society* (Penguin, 1967), p. 99

44 Fraser, op. cit., p. 69

45 http://news.bbc.co.uk/1/hi/uk_politics/2592745.stm

46 Fraser, op. cit., p. 90

47 http://www.civitas.org.uk/data/prisonTooMany.php

48 http://www.civitas.org.uk/data/twoCountries.php

49 Fraser, op. cit., p. 100

50 *The Times*, 18 July 2008

51 Ibid.

52 http://www.theatlantic.com/doc/198203/broken-windows

53 Fraser, op. cit., p. 278

54 Ibid., p. 20

55 *Guardian*, 17 June 2008

8: FOOTBALL

1 Greg Dyke, *Inside Story* (Harper Perennial, 2005), p. 226

2 Ibid., p. 227

3 Ibid., p. 231

4 Ibid., p. 232

5 Ibid., p. 232

6 http://news.bbc.co.uk/sport1/hi/football/europe/6280032.stm

7 *Observer*, 3 December 2006

9: JIHADIST ISLAM

1   http://www.guardian.co.uk/books/1989/feb/18/
    fiction.salmanrushdie
2   *New York Times*, 19 February 1989
3   *New York Times,* 20 February 1989
4   http://www.danielpipes.org/article/301
5   http://www.danielpipes.org/article/186
6   *Observer*, 11 January 2009
7   http://www.tomgrossmedia.com/mideastdispatches/archives/
    000393.html
8   http://news.bbc.co.uk/1/hi/world/europe/4660796.stm
9   *Muslim News*, 30 August 1996
10 http://news.bbc.co.uk/1/hi/uk/4166402.stm
11 http://www.prospect-magazine.co.uk/article_details.
    php?id=7980
12 http://www.memri.org/bin/articles.cgi?Page=archives&
    Area=sr&ID=SR3004
13 http://www.memri.org/bin/articles.cgi?Page=archives&
    Area=sd&ID=SP24601
14 http://www.mcb.org.uk/library/article_02-04-04.php
15 *The Times*, 11 August 2005
16 http://www.telegraph.co.uk/news/uknews/1496621/Top-job-
    fighting-extremism-for-Muslim-who-praised-bomber.html
17 Ibid.
18 http://news.bbc.co.uk/1/hi/uk/6980888.stm
19 http://memri.org/bin/articles.cgi?Area=sr&ID=SR01102
20 http://www.timesonline.co.uk/tol/news/uk/article687513.
    ece
21 http://news.bbc.co.uk/1/hi/scotland/glasgow_and_west/
    7519040.stm
22 http://www.independent.co.uk/opinion/leading-
    articles/leading-article-the-archbishop-has-stepped-into-a-
    political-and-intellectual- minefield-780233.html

23 *Daily Telegraph*, 16 September 2008
24 Ibid.
25 *Sunday Telegraph*, 19 February 2006
26 http://www.guardian.co.uk/commentisfree/2006/jul/09/
terrorism.religion

10: THE FAMILY

1 Christine Wallace, *Greer: Untamed Shrew* (John Blake, 1997), p. 87
2 *Guardian*, 7 March 1999
3 Germaine Greer, *The Female Eunuch* (Harper, 1970)
4 *New York Times*, 22 March 1971
5 *Guardian*, 7 March 1999
6 *Daily Telegraph*, 9 July 2008
7 *Daily Mail*, 13 December 2007
8 *Sunday Times*, 4 March 2007
9 *Sunday Times*, 3 December 2006

INDEX

NOTE ON THE AUTHOR

Stephen Pollard is currently Editor of the *Jewish Chronicle*, has written columns for several publications including *The Times* and the *Daily Mail* and maintained a lively *Spectator* blog. He is also the author of the controversial 2004 biography of David Blunkett, and co-authored with Andrew Adonis *A Class Act: The Myth of Britain's Classless Society*, which was shortlisted for the Orwell Prize.

Croft 10/10
CLARE 6/12
Fap 6/14
SGR 9/14
COR 3/16
VDH 5/16
C G 6/17
AWK 18